YOUR PUPPY
AND HOW TO TRAIN HIM

YOUR PUPPY

AND HOW TO TRAIN HIM

Huldine V. Beamish

FABER AND FABER LTD
24 Russell Square
London

First published in mcmlvii
by Faber and Faber Limited
24 Russell Square London WC1
First published in this edition mcmlxiii
Reprinted mcmlxviii
Printed in Great Britain by
Latimer Trend & Co Ltd Whitstable
All rights reserved

TO
ALL MY DOGS—
PAST AND PRESENT—
WHO HAVE TAUGHT ME
THE LITTLE I KNOW

CONTENTS

CONTENTS

ILLUSTRATIONS

———

ACKNOWLEDGEMENTS

Some of the photographs in this book were taken with the kind co-operation of the well-known trainer, Mr. R. M. Montgomery, of Worplesdon, Surrey. I should like to thank the following for permission to reproduce their photographs: The Sport and General Press Agency Ltd. (frontispiece); Thomas Fall (plates 1, 3, 4, 13 and 16), and C. M. Cooke (plates 9 and 14).

INTRODUCTION

——❧——

'Yes,' said Father Brown, 'I always like a dog,
so long as he isn't spelt backwards.'

G. K. CHESTERTON

(The Incredulity of Father Brown)

I must explain that the following book is not written for
the perusal of my friend with the established kennel, nor
for my colleague who trains his own dogs and sometimes
other people's as well. It is primarily written for you who
either possess that exacting responsibility, a puppy for the
first time, or to you who have always owned a dog of some
sort, but never seem to understand much about him nor,
above all, his quite complicated mentality.

The kind of dog who has inspired this book is far more
universal than is generally supposed. He is really rather un-
speakable. I meet him everywhere, in other people's houses,
in the street, the fields, and garden. He shocks me by his bad
manners, horrible behaviour, and complete lack of control.
Sometimes I wonder why his owner has a dog at all. He
doesn't deserve one, he doesn't do him justice. It's unfair to
blame the dog. Yet the owner's complete ignorance of the
canine mind can be extremely irritating, and the resulting
lack of canine manners is somewhat deplorable. Perhaps the
solution lies in the fact that the majority of dog-owners

merely sit down and accept the fact that dogs were made just like that, and nothing will alter it.

I am so often asked how I make my dogs do this and that —why they are so well-behaved and quiet when they stay in other people's houses, and how on earth I manage to teach them their various accomplishments. So I'm going to make a few suggestions. You see, your dog will never be popular if you don't teach him something about manners. There are heaps of non-doggy people who are willing to be converted, but naturally feel repugnance when your dog jumps all over them, or is sick in their car, or bounces through their best flower-bed.

I hope to show you that these things need not be, and that you can impress your friends and acquaintances far better by a well-behaved dog who has perhaps learnt a few useful accomplishments.

You may think your own special dog hasn't much of a brain. Believe me, he has. And you may be pleasantly surprised to find what you can do with this receptive and susceptible instrument. Why not try?

Chapter 1

THE QUESTION OF
INTELLIGENCE

Intelligence or Reasoning Power?

As I'm far more interested in the psychology and behaviour of your dog than in his appearance or physical attractions, a little should be said on the subject of this mind of his. Can a dog think or reason? Does he possess intelligence? It is a much-debated question, but one which I find has various grades of followers. It is significant that the most heated supporters of the naturally-a-dog-can-think faction are to be found among old maids, soft-hearted people who 'love' dogs, and people who are admittedly ignorant about science, natural history, and zoology. You know the kind of thing I mean—you may even have said something like it yourself. 'Of course dear doggie thinks. Look at his sweet face; you can see it.' This is the same person who tells you solemnly that dogs go to heaven. But at the other end of the argument sits the scientist, cool, full of facts, proofs, tests. He it is who keeps cages of guinea-pigs and white rats, who rings a bell when the food is ready, and watches the reaction of animal mentality, the pace of assimilation from one generation to another. No, he's not at all childish; he knows far more than we shall ever know. He hasn't much feeling for dogs as individuals, but he is vitally interested in the

15

mind of the animal that man has civilized most successfully. His tests have been really rather disappointing, and go to prove that the dog is, after all, only an animal, which is what one might expect, in spite of the assurances of hysterical spinsters—'But he's almost *human*, you know.'

Well then, let me plunge bravely into this controversial subject, and say at once that I personally have come to the reluctant conclusion that the dog has no intelligence at all, or none that matters. What is intelligence? My rather inadequate dictionary says, somewhat shortly, 'Mental power', which one may take to mean reasoning, thinking, planning power; the sort of power that, in my humble opinion, puts man on a different plane from that of any other animal. That is intelligence. Animals have plenty of qualities to make up for this lack, dogs perhaps above all, and I think it is mistaking these qualities which has led to a misuse of the word 'intelligence'.

The dog's apparent intelligence (reasoning, thinking, planning power) is really a combination of four chief qualities. They are, in order of importance: Natural Instinct, Habits, Training, and Experience. Actually this brings us to a deeper question altogether—the realization of an undisputed fact, the mysterious gap dividing purely animal mentality from the purely human. Animal mentality is limited: it has arrived practically at the end of its development and growth, and can hardly, in any circumstances, be expected to progress much further. Whereas, of course, human mentality always progresses, never stops, never goes back. It is a collective and general movement: individual backslidings don't count; the development goes on all the time. There's no limit to this progress as far as can be seen.

Just as the anthropoids remained apes while human beings developed beyond, so the rest of the animal world stands, a vast living monument to the everlasting wonder of evolutionary creation. Every stage of development can be found in the world of to-day, from the single cell which increases by merely dividing itself, to the ever-progressive human being, whose physical evolution is already slowly changing to something greater. But remember, always remember, dogs are animals, however much we make them our friends, our companions, however many tears we waste on their all too frequent graves.

I can't help knowing that the dog's reasoning powers are practically non-existent, that he has no real intelligence. My own dogs frequently perform some quite amazing things; they surprise even me. But on the other hand the cleverest of them will do something so utterly stupid, so blatantly idiotic, that I am bound to realize there must be complete lack of thought; and then I remember the dog is only an animal, with all an animal's limitations.

Let's have a simple example of this so-called intelligence. A man gives his dog a penny; the dog goes off to the news-agent and brings back the paper. 'What an intelligent dog!' we all say. But he isn't. If anyone deserves credit, it's the owner, who has taught the dog to carry—created a habit. The dog merely received an order and obeyed it because he was taught to do so.

I think the chief characteristic in a dog is instinct, the subtle development and exploitations of which can be so easily confused with genuine reasoning power. And the second consideration in canine mentality is habit. You've no idea, until you train dogs extensively, how much can be achieved by habit. I suppose habit is the one factor that counts above all in training. Just as you can instil good or useful habits, so bad ones may be as easily picked up. It's all rather amusing. You train your baby into habits, and try not to let him assimilate or start bad ones, even later, as he grows older. Think of the immense trouble taken over a

17

baby's habits. But what about the young dog? Don't you realize that the two mentalities are the same, only the dog develops with less fuss? I shouldn't mind betting I'd make my puppy clean in the house before you'd do the same with your baby. After all, the canine tribe never soil their beds by choice, and it's a well-known fact you can't ever house-train monkeys! So why not apply a little of the trouble you give to your child with eager parental care to that badly behaved dog of yours? He'd improve, and heaven knows there's room for it.

About training I shall have a good deal to say later on, and as a contributing substitute for that non-existent intelligence—or reasoning power—it plays a very large part. Without training, dogs would be just rather crude wild animals, no better than wolves, coyotes, or jackals. As it is, you can achieve apparent miracles by using the dog's natural instincts, taking advantage of them, and coaxing them into performances useful to yourself.

Experience comes with the years, and is another important reason why we mistakenly call dogs intelligent. It's mostly memory, the experience of cause and effect, things noticed by the dog over a long period. For a dog undoubtedly possesses a memory, sometimes a better one than we have ourselves. What makes the setter or spaniel go every time to a certain clump of rushes? The memory of a bird or rabbit he once found there. Experience is extremely useful in all working dogs, and we are frequently apt to expect too much from a young one, when actually he hasn't had the time to learn what to do in given circumstances.

The Substitutes

So, in proving that a dog doesn't possess any uncanny or miraculous or human intelligence, we have discovered four valuable substitutes: Instinct, Habit, Training, and Experience. These are enough to make us credit him with far more mental power than he actually possesses, and all his actions are based on those four qualities; they can account for nearly everything. We should remember that animals, limited as they are, have compensations. If you or I were shut in a dark box, railed off to some obscure place a hundred miles away, seeing nothing of our journey, we should be lost if we tried to go back. But the dog isn't lost, and most animals and birds can find their way back. It looks like a miracle, and is in reality an excellent example of the kind of instinct—developed complicated instinct—with which animals are blessed.

Once a Scottish farmer bought some sheep at a market many miles away from his farm. The way home led over moorlands and hills, with scarcely a track to go by. The man ordered his dog to take the newly bought sheep back to the farm. And the dog covered all those miles of wild moorland with the sheep, bringing them safely home. Possibly he met other sheep on the hills; his own charges may have tried to mix with them or break away. But finally all were delivered intact at the farm. Intelligent? Of course not. The dog was merely obeying his deeply rooted herding instinct, coupled with the habits acquired through his master's training, his experience helping him to bring home the identical sheep with which he started. Just as well-trained collies can drive any single sheep pointed out to them, so this one obeyed his instincts, habits, training, and experience. Naturally only a superlatively trained dog could perform such a feat, so let the credit go to his master.

A retriever, having seen and marked a wounded bird falling, is sent to gather it. Guided by his eyes, he goes at full gallop to the place where the bird fell, but when he reaches it, the bird has run away through the brambles. So at once he uses his nose on the line, follows the bird, catches it, and brings it back. There is no actual reasoning power in this; it is a matter of instinct and training.

Take a very young puppy out in the long grass. Show him a nice bit of smelly meat: holding him with one hand, throw the meat into the grass when you know he's watching. Then let him go. He rushes off to where he saw—or thought he saw—the meat fall, and if his eyes deceived him a little, he immediately and unthinkingly puts his nose to the ground. This is inherited instinct, an instinct which probably started before we ourselves had shed our tails!

Even a greyhound, whose powers of scent have been bred away almost to nothing, will, when unsighted from his quarry, do his best to find the scent with his nose. He doesn't succeed, but you won't get him to drop this now useless instinctive action. He hasn't the intelligence to know it's no good: only long experience will teach him that.

I suppose nowhere is instinct more pronounced than in a bitch with puppies, or indeed any breeding animal. Here we must definitely bow to that most wonderful display of natural laws, though still thrusting away the fetish of intelligence, of reasoning power. The cleverness doesn't exist in the animals themselves, but in that highly complicated and intricate mystery—nature.

The bitch who is about to have a family takes care of herself, gradually calms down in her movements, and changes her habits. She makes a bed as far as possible from other animals, and prepares that bed before the family arrives. But remember, she isn't human, she doesn't *know* she's going to have a family until after the first arrival. *Her* mother never told her about the facts of life. This preparation is no more than the instinct that makes a bird build a nest, or the rabbit prepare her burrow by pulling fur from her own breast.

20

What utter fools are human beings in these matters beside animals! The bitch with puppies doesn't have to be told and taught what to do with them, how to clean and feed them; she just knows. She keeps them all in spotless condition, the nest beautifully clean, and she is ready at any moment to defend them, even from her own master. But the bitch isn't intelligent to do all this; the credit for these things must be looked for elsewhere.

To the whole animal world the secrets are given. Invariably the raven builds his nest on a ledge which no one can reach, except by artificial means, from either the top or bottom of the cliff. It's generally placed under an overhanging rock to make attack even more difficult. Most birds follow this plan, and it's incredibly easy to miss a nest altogether unless a very careful search is undertaken. But there's no forethought about this, no intelligence, no reasoning power. Just inherited instinct.

Instinct and the Brain

So the dog's actions and mentality are guided by the same impulse, in greater or less degree. Furthermore, it's far easier than may be supposed to breed in an instinct which was previously non-existent in the ancestors of any particular strain, by which I mean making the puppies of a herding breed—as an instance—instinctively retrieve after a few generations have done so. The collie pup, bred from parents who have worked sheep, and whose ancestors did the same, will start herding poultry or sheep or even other dogs as soon as he can run about. Actually I think the sheepdog is the best example of inherited instinct. The retriever puppy should retrieve naturally from an early age. But in an incredibly few generations you can produce spontaneous instincts which were originally not natural to the breed of dog.

For instance, you could train a particularly suitable collie for gun-work. His progeny would be more easily trained, and finally the strain you created would work and start work by instinct as soon as they were physically able to do so. I have proved this fact quite definitely in my own dogs. This principle applies also in the other direction, and instinctive work can be just as easily bred out as in, if the individuals of each generation are not asked to do the work for which they were originally intended.

There are few limits to training. If people took the trouble they could teach their dogs the most amazing and spectacular achievements, provided the dog was asked only to perform duties suited to his conformation. The dog's thinking is mainly a matter of cause and effect, memory and experience. An escaped wolf, caught once in a trap, will never forget the connections with that experience, and is extremely unlikely to be caught again. His nose, feelings, sense of danger will all warn him in another such situation. A young terrier will chase rabbits right up to where he sees them disappear into their holes. He remains sniffing there, wondering how he can get them out. This dog continues the habit for some years, but later on, when his muzzle turns grey and his eyes aren't as good as they were and he's probably a little deaf, he still hunts rabbits because he enjoys it. When he knows they are making straight for the burrow, he stops and lets them go, not taking the trouble to attempt what he knows is impossible. There is no intelligence about this, no particular thought. In his lifetime he has seen so many rabbits escape that way, he understands at last he can never be as quick as they are, or reach them in time.

Naturally the canine mental gifts vary tremendously with the individual in exactly the same way that people themselves vary. Particular breeds possess special qualities; some are quick to learn, others not worth the trouble of training. If you want your dog to be useful, then you must choose a representative from a working breed, or at least one whose inanity doesn't stare you in the face every time you look at his empty countenance.

You may say you only want your dog as a companion or a pet. Yes, but why not choose a sensible one while you're about it? You may imagine your present dog is satisfactory in this role, yet he leaves, I think, much to be desired. I compare his mentality to that of my own choice, and find him sadly lacking. True, I've trained mine, and you've done nothing at all with yours. He doesn't even know how to sit quietly when you tell him; he's just his jolly doggy self. But before you consider another dog, do be careful to choose one that is trainable.

You may tell me I'm only quibbling and playing with words when I talk of the four substitutes for intelligence. Then let me tell you that if the dog was possessed of *real* intelligence—such as we have—you couldn't train him at all. He'd be far too clever, and when an animal becomes too clever for the human being, he can be of no practical use to that being.

Admittedly the dog, in common with the child, has a brain. It's entirely up to you to help him develop to his limit, or leave that brain dormant all his life. He'll be far more happy if you give him something to do, something to think about, something to perform. You'll be amazed at the satisfaction you derive from teaching him, and watching your lessons bear fruit. I don't care whether you live in a flat or a caravan, a farm or a London house; if you have a dog at all, give him a chance to use his natural and acquired talents, thereby enjoying his life to the full.

The whole trouble with many dogs of the larger breeds who are forced to lead a confined life is not so much lack of exercise, which they can forgo as well as a man who works

23

every day at a desk, but lack of brain employment; the talents they might have shown are frequently degraded into idle, harmful habits, for which they are duly chided. An Alsatian, unless he is old and experienced and resigned, will tear up anything within reach if he is confined for long. Yes, because his brain is idle, and he must do something. Instead of punishing him, take him out on the lawn and give him a few simple lessons. You'll find he'll settle down quite contentedly after them, and probably go to sleep. Mental exercise can be just as tiring as miles of walking.

It never occurs to you that your dog's brain is an unexplored mine, whose treasures you have never seen. Why not take a voyage of discovery, and see what you can find? But do explore the right mine; so many are practically worthless. Happily, buying or breeding a dog isn't like marriage. If you do happen to choose an unsuitable one, you can soon remedy the mistake. Don't just give up with a sigh, and say, 'Dogs will be dogs'; because dogs, above all animals, are so much what human beings want them to be.

Chapter 2

BUYING A PUPPY

Choosing Brains

Much ink has been spilt on the subject of buying a puppy, but nearly always from the physical point of view. If you are a breeder and show enthusiast, you must generally choose your puppy with the idea of having the best-looking animal in the litter, irrespective of sense, quickness of brain, or trainability.

You, who want a companion dog, and I who want one to work—the two requirements should be much the same—are seeking something more than physical appearance, so long as the puppy is sound and reasonably presentable. Very well, we'll go and look at a litter, say about eight weeks old. They're all playing about happily in their run, quite at home and thoroughly natural. This is the best way to see puppies. Spend as long as possible watching them; then go into the run. See which ones are friendly, which suspicious, or which actually nervous. The one who is the most lively and jumps up, ruining all your clothes, is probably the best from our point of view. Keep your eye on the one who worries the others all the time, and never keeps still. Choose the boldest, the naughtiest, and probably the dirtiest. Don't be misled by that dear little pathetic face that sits in the background, not sure whether to run away or not. And the one with a 'sensible' face, whose expression might really be one of calm stupidity. You can clap your hands suddenly, and watch the result. The bold puppy will stop to see where the sound came from, full of curiosity, and then probably rush at you again. The most timid will run away and hide in the kennel, peeping out later to see if all's clear, really rather ashamed of himself. You might throw something, a bone or a bit of stick, and see if any of them picks it up, and if so, which.

Before you came at all, you had already decided whether you wanted a dog or a bitch. Now this is a question I can never understand, and only one of the many fallacies people foster about dogs. Let's remember again that you want an easily trained companion, and I want a worker. Nearly everyone like *you* will choose a dog if you can afford the higher price. I wonder why. I've always wondered why. When I ask, you invariably say, 'Oh, bitches are such a nuisance; they have to be shut up.' That is, if you are doggish enough to put it like that. Most likely, you just look at me with rather a silly face and mumble that you always thought it was better to have a dog. Well, you're wrong, either way. Let me tell you a few facts. Bitches are nearly always more affectionate, more loyal, and more devoted than dogs. They are generally far quicker in the brain, and therefore easier to teach. As a rule they don't fight, and don't want to. Above all, they are never worried or led astray by their sexual needs if properly looked after. At an absolute maximum they have to be confined for six weeks out of the fifty-two, and no one could grumble at that. You generally know when these times are due, and are prepared accordingly.

Dogs, on the other hand, are more aggressive by nature; they're more interested in other dogs—and bitches. There's no time during the whole year that a dog won't take notice of a bitch when she's interesting (or even when she isn't), and he'll follow her in preference to following you. If he has to work on ground where a bitch or another dog has left a signature, he must fully investigate that before he'll continue working. Unless a dog is particularly well brought up, his sex is worrying him all the time, even on a walk, when he must show everyone he has passed along. In my opinion, the average dog is more bother than he's worth, even though there are, of course, many exceptions. A dog can contract many bad habits which never tempt a bitch at all: these are mainly concerned with his everlasting sex, which apparently he can never forget. In fact he's always sex-conscious. In any case, it's rather fun to breed your own puppies, whereas it's not nearly the same to look for a wife for your dog.

However, you can be obstinate if you like, and have your dog. I should choose a bitch every time from a practical point of view. Incidentally, the dogs who are carefully picked and chosen and trained to lead the blind are *almost invariably* bitches, which more or less proves what I am trying to say.

By this time we've chosen our puppies. The reason why I take the liveliest and most bouncing one is that you can restrain high spirits, and turn them into good working qualities. They usually show stamina and staying power, energy, and a capacity for work. You can divert high spirits and liveliness into more serious channels, but you can't coax these qualities into that silly, nervous puppy who sits in the background, or peeps round the kennel door. When you have to correct or punish, the lively, jolly puppy recovers almost immediately, though remembering the crime and its consequence. The other may sulk for some time; he may run away, and be quite useless for further training until he gets over it. You can curb high spirits, but you can't create them.

Choosing a puppy from a litter you have bred yourself is far easier than buying from someone else. You look for the qualities you want most, and have unlimited time to sit among the litter and watch them. It must be remembered though, that puppies, like young children, are extremely deceptive, both in character and appearance. Actually you can't know what your dog will be like until he has acquired his second teeth. Very often, a bitch puppy will change her character completely about the first time she comes in season, or just before. This applies to appearance as well as character, and of the larger breeds it's not safe to call a puppy beautiful, a certain champion, and so forth, until he's a year old. There have been many disappointments over this change. Your puppy may promise well at twelve weeks, and at eight months he may have grown too big, leggy, and all sorts of other lurking horrors!

However, although his character concerns us more than his shape, let's remember that a nice-looking, well-bred dog doesn't cost any more to feed than a mongrel. I have a prejudice against mongrels, and would never keep one by choice. It's quite unnecessary, and is in direct opposition to all efforts for improvement in live stock; though here again there are a few exceptions, and very occasionally people deliberately breed mongrels for some set purpose and plan, which is permissible if scientifically done.

Taking the Puppy Home

Well, then, we've chosen our eight-weeks-old puppies for better or worse, and eight weeks is quite a good age, as we can bring them up as we want from the beginning. I shall now follow you home, and see what you do with yours. To start with, he's sick in the car, and instead of being the bright, happy little thing you took from his brothers and sisters, you see a miserable whining animal, and wonder if he'll ever be jolly again. You look at the mess on the seat of the car and feel a little annoyed. Enthusiasm is slightly damped. However, you've got your puppy and must make the best of it, even though a sense of responsibility now sits on your shoulders quite suddenly, and you wonder if you'll ever manage to bring him up properly.

You arrive home. Have you made any preparations for the puppy's arrival? No, not many. You've decided, of course, that he's to live in the house, and you must therefore house-train him as soon as possible. The car is put away, and you carry the new arrival, slightly bedraggled from his car-sick experiences, into the house. Everyone must come and see him. By this time a little of his good spirits have reasserted themselves, and he's quite willing to play. During a pause in these capers he goes off round the carpet, sniffing. You merely watch him with a proud smile, and when he does what he intended to do on your best carpet, you rush at him *after* the harm's done, probably rub his nose in the approved fashion, at the same time giving him a smack. Then perhaps you put him out, or let him go to sleep in your favourite arm-chair.

Yes, but if you'd thought for a moment, he'd never have spoilt the carpet at all. You shouldn't have carried him in from the car, but made him run about outside until he'd done everything of which a puppy is capable. Then, and only then, would he have been fit to go into the house for a time, and a very short time at that.

But I can explain this better if you come home with me and my new puppy, and see what I do. In the first place, owing to many bitter and sad experiences, I've brought a box to put mine in when she travels in the car. I've always hated dogs in a car in any circumstances, because I like cars. To my mind the last word in crime is to let a puppy soil the upholstery by being sick all over it. A box is quite easily brought, the puppy shut in. She'll shriek at the top of her voice, of course, but I don't mind that, because I know that

29

if I drive at a good average speed she'll soon be too busy with other matters to be able to shriek. Sure enough, the voice dies down, and sweet silence reigns. We arrive home, and I give her a run on the grass. I am assuming for the moment that I, like you, have only this puppy, and no other dogs at all. (Would it were true!)

When I've finished playing about with her, and have other things to do, I don't take her into the house. No thank you. She goes into a nice kennel already prepared with a beautiful deep bed of straw, a bowl of water, and a bone. After closing the door, I don't go off straight away, but stay near by, out of sight and—just as important—out of scent. The puppy finds herself alone. She misses her brothers and sisters, and the nice, kind person who has just been playing with her. If she's the greedy sort—and I hope she is—she'll fall on the bone and forget everything else for a time. And when that's finished, she may go to sleep. I sincerely hope so. More likely, as soon as the door is shut, she'll start whining, then barking, and finally howling. With somewhat fearsome noises I rush to the door, fling it open, cry 'Shut up!' or some such expression, and give her a smack. She looks at me with a wondering face. I shut the door and pretend to disappear. In a second or so the noise starts again, and I have to go back and treat it in the same way. Perhaps I may waste half an hour doing this, no matter how pressing anything else may be. Finally the puppy becomes tired, and goes to sleep. For a time the noise is over.

This, for the puppy, is one of the first experiences of cause and effect. It corresponds almost exactly with the treatment of a young baby lying in its cot. Though there's nothing actually wrong with the baby, it's discontented at being put to bed, and would far prefer to be swayed about and amused in someone's arms. Therefore it protests with a loud, wearisome, and tedious voice. Surely it's the greatest mistake,

almost a crime of upbringing, to go and pander to this protest? In addition, it becomes more difficult next time to put
the baby to sleep. Anyone who lifts a healthy but discontented baby from its cot just because of the noise is making
the same fatal mistake as the owner who lets out his puppy
or dog when it chooses to whine or scream.

Later on, probably in the evening, I come back with a
feed. If the puppy is quiet, I let her out, give her the food,
and tell her she's a good child. But if she's howling when I
arrive, I put the food aside for a few minutes, administer the
shut-up treatment once more until she stays silent when the
door's closed, after which she can be let out, praised, and
fed. I make it an invariable rule to walk the puppy about
until all natural requirements have had expression. In this
way I create an early habit which continues through the
dog's later life.

Now for a few reasons and arguments. I think most
people are foolish to start house-training a puppy at the
early age of eight weeks. It's expecting far too much of a
young creature which is, after all, only a baby. You must
remember that all young animals have to relieve themselves
many times during the day, and during the night as well.
Unless you are prepared and have the time to watch your
puppy all day long, why not put off his house-training until
his physical habits are a little less in evidence? Puppies must
eat several times a day, and have corresponding needs,
whereas the adult dog should only eat once, and at the most
his bowels move twice a day, morning and evening. By all
means have your puppy in the house at times, but only when
you know it's safe, and when you can watch him all the
time for the easily detected signs.

Remember another important item in the young puppy's
schedule. He must sleep a good deal. While he sleeps, he's
digesting his meals, and growing. Don't deprive him of a

moment's sleep; don't go on playing with him when you see he doesn't want to play any longer. The younger the puppy the more frequent his very vital naps, so let him have them in peace. And when he wakes up, you can guess the first thing he'll want to do, can't you? Hurry him out!

Settling Down

Personally, I seldom start keeping a puppy in the house until it is four or six months old, and even that's early enough, though the process is a gradual one. It's worth far more *never to let your puppy offend in the house* than to punish him for doing so. Dogs are strange creatures, and they generally develop very definite habits. If a puppy has always gone on the grass, gravel, earth, or paving-stones at these times, he looks about for these things again, and hesitates and is uncomfortable about offending elsewhere. You can make most dogs treat their kennel as a house if you have sufficient patience, and set about it the right way.

I shall have more to say about house-training later on, when your puppy is older, but meanwhile let's get back to him now. Since having his evening meal he has probably committed a greater crime than ever, because you didn't think there was any special hurry to put him out. Where's he going to sleep? There's a box in the kitchen, and it won't matter so much if he makes a mess on the kitchen floor. Right, put him in his box. He immediately gets out and runs after you as you leave. You take him back gently. This is repeated until you get tired of it, and rush out quickly, hoping for the best. But you couldn't have smacked the poor little thing instead of patting it, could' you? You couldn't have caught him firmly by the scruff of his neck, and scoldingly kept him in his box? You wouldn't have raised your voice to him, or anything like that? Well, it's your funeral.

1. Full of curiosity
(*p. 26*)

2. Why not choose
a sensible one?
(*p. 23*)

3. Dear jolly little selves (*p. 35*)

4. A full-time job (*p. 40*)

5. This jumping-up habit (*p. 42*)

6. Firmly to a post (*p. 46*)

7. A sharp pull (*p. 48*)

8. Coming in of her own accord (*p. 48*)

10. The floor instead of the seats (*p.* 67)

9. A slack lead (*p.* 49)

11. Stops beside me (*p. 70*)

12. In a circle round him (*p. 72*)

13. Communal training (*p. 99*)

14. A well-behaved dog (*p. 122*)

15. Foods and feeding (*p. 123*)

16. The really healthy dog (*p. 146*)

You go to bed to the accompaniment of screams and howls from the lower regions. If you can sleep soundly, all will be well, and the puppy will tire himself out. But you think he might keep someone else awake. People might grumble. Besides, the dear thing is unhappy. So you go down and open the kitchen door. The puppy rushes out, delighted that his screams brought someone to keep him company, and equally delighted when you stroke or pat him. In his own mind he notes that his noisy protest has succeeded, resulting in caresses—a very fatal deduction. You decide he'll be quiet if he goes up to your own bedroom, and be hanged to the mess in the morning. And, further pandering to this tiresome child, you let him lie at the end of the bed, or in your chair, or anywhere he pleases, so long as he's quiet. Your present motto—and the very worst in training animals or children—is 'Anything for a quiet life'.

What a pity! And how regrettable. Because in a dog's education you must never let him have the better of you; he must never think he's been clever enough to avoid this and that because you're too lazy to go on longer than he can. Believe me, dogs can be as obstinate as anything else; they can wear you out and try your patience to its limits. But if you're going to be successful, you must never let them metaphorically smile to themselves over your defeat. When they do wrong, they must be made to see it, and vice versa. Praise is more valuable if it's not given all the time. Don't be nice to a puppy even as an indirect consequence of bad behaviour. Though actual punishment may not be necessary, you can withhold the caresses he likes so much. He'll soon know why.

The next night will probably be a repetition of the previous one, and life goes on, and you give up trying to make your puppy sleep in the kitchen by himself when he likes your bed so much better. You don't realize that even in this apparently small matter you've laid the foundations of a sloppy education, to result finally in the somewhat badly behaved dog you have now.

Meanwhile, my puppy has been howling too. But every evening when I put her in her kennel, I stay outside and wait for the whine to start, always applying the shut-up treatment, always using the same words, tones, and actions. In a few days my puppy has learnt the first lesson of keeping silent, and sleeping by herself. Yours won't even stay by himself in a room without kicking up a fuss. He finds the fuss pays, whereas mine found the fuss produced rather disagreeable or painful results. See the difference?

Chapter 3

FIRST LESSONS

Discipline and Training

Now puppies are extremely like all children and most grown-ups. They are their dear, jolly little selves as long as they can do what they like whenever they like. Life is sweet without discipline; tempers and temperaments are sweet too, and for the individuals in question the world is a lovely place. It won't do, all the same. You want—or I hope you do—your dog to be at least a decent member of society, just as you hope your child will be. And neither of them will become that unless or until a good deal of discipline has been instilled. Discipline doesn't mean giving orders. It means seeing those orders are carried out, whether it's pleasant for you or not.

Training of any sort tends to change character, sometimes with unprofitable results. But if the puppy or child is sound to start with, they'll stand any amount of discipline of the right sort, without—and this is important—losing their individuality. You don't want to make dogs mechanical, although a good deal of their training must necessarily be so. They have times of relaxation and times of work as every civilized being should, in order to lead a balanced and justified life.

Training a dog doesn't so much mean suppressing his

natural tendencies as directing those tendencies into useful channels. Substituting independence of spirit for a somewhat slavish attitude is in a dog more of a blessing than a curse, because the really independent dog is of no practical use to human beings. It is not creative, as human independence generally is.

I suppose the time has come when I must rather wearily repeat the most desirable qualities of the ideal trainer. You can read of them in every book on the subject, so you know without my telling you that you have to possess calmness, an equable temper, and unlimited patience. Yes, but you don't know that though *you* may possess all these qualities —how enviable!—you can't train your dog even to sit properly. And I, who have none of the required characteristics (except perhaps a measure of patience) can train my dogs to do almost anything. Why is this?

I'll tell you something. Trainers of animals are born, not made. And when they've employed this inborn gift for many years, they gradually learn things about animal psychology, things which can never really be expressed in writing. It's just an inner knowledge, almost an instinct, which can't be bought or learnt in five minutes, or five months, or even five years. I suppose everything to do with animals is like that.

So you see it's unfortunate that you may have the stipulated temperament, but no knowledge, and I have the knowledge, but not the necessary qualities. I do comfort myself, however, that every animal I train teaches me more patience, more calmness, and less exasperation. Animals are so good for you: restraint is always necessary, and often makes a vital difference between success and failure. Because in training there must be no failure, only success.

Then there's the question of cruelty. Ignorant people tell me they hate circuses because so much cruelty is practised in training the performing animals. This is a stupid statement. Almost every animal in a circus is trained by kindness and persuasion and perhaps edible rewards. To my mind a circus is interesting as the superlative demonstration of what man can do with animals. You see, the main reason for not being cruel is that it simply doesn't pay. You never gain anything by it, apart from any ethical point of view. Just as 'honesty is the best policy', so is kindness in training animals. And if you happen to lose your temper and do things you should never do, well, you're the loser, every time. It may take weeks to blot out your mistake, your technical crime. Indeed, you may never manage to make the animal forget that you forgot.

A multitude of difference exists between firmness and cruelty—calmly administered punishment, and a wild fury. Quite often the dog should be punished, but you must do it calmly, even though you are giving him a thrashing, which should be reserved for only one or two crimes. There are plenty of methods of punishment, and often a moral thrashing is quite as effective as a physical one. Punishment should only be given on certain occasions, but always when the dog has deliberately done wrong, knowing he has done so. It would be absurd to give him a thrashing for mere ignorance.

It's terribly easy to sit here and glibly write of what you should or should not do. But not so easy to remember when your dog is crouching, ears back, obstinate-faced, refusing to look for something you know is there and have asked him to find. It's easy to advocate a calm, unruffled hiding when he lies, looking like some angel, among the torn and bleeding corpses of your favourite hens. Or when, at the sound of the first shot, he rushes off across the root-field, gaily putting up the coveys as he goes. Can you be calm then? Is your hand steady as you lift the leather when you finally get him? I know mine isn't!

House and Kennel Training

It's time we got back to our respective puppies. I think I've noticed you make a few mistakes already, but that's nothing to what you may do, so we might as well talk a little about house-training.

If you're determined to keep your very young puppy in the house from the beginning, it's far more difficult. But it can be done, and the chief thing to remember is to take the puppy outside at frequent regular intervals, and always after a meal, which is the most important time. Don't be careless about this, or lazy. I know it'll be cold one night, or wet, and after shivering for several minutes while the puppy sits and looks at you, you'll probably go in, hoping for the best. But don't. Walk him round until he has done all he should. It's well worth it: every time he performs outside is a step gained. You're instilling a habit, and a healthy desire for using grass instead of carpets. It's quite a good plan to take him where he's been before; it always seems to bring light to an otherwise limited understanding. So, with this constant vigilance, your puppy will eventually become house-trained, and his habits as regular as his meals should be.

Personally I should never attempt this early introduction to the house. My puppy has to learn a lot of things before she is privileged to share my room. All her preliminary house-training is really done while she still lives in the kennel; and when I see the kennel clean every morning for about a fortnight, I can then safely keep her in the house at night. There's no fuss, no rushing about, flinging doors open, mopping with a floor-cloth, or watching the puppy all the time. Then, too, she has learnt the restriction of a lead, she has learnt to lie down quietly when tied up, and so on. It might be as well here to explain how to train an older puppy.

There's a very awkward time from the age of about two months to four. Puppies are having perhaps three or four meals a day, growing very rapidly, and seem to possess an incredible amount of waste matter which must somehow and somewhere be expelled. It's mainly for this reason that I keep my puppy outside until she has reached the age of five or six months, by which time she is only having two meals a day, and her frequent physical needs are abating.

I make every effort I can to see she is put to bed in the kennel with all duties performed, and I try to be out early to save at least some mishap in the morning. Even then, the kennel will be dirtied during the night for some time. By degrees this lessens, habits are induced, and the puppy looks and waits for the walk over her chosen spots rather than perform in the kennel. By this time she has grown used to being tied up, and I try the experiment of fastening her rather shortly to her bed or bench for the night. Now dogs are clean animals by nature—they loathe fouling their bed—and so my puppy, finding she can't get away far enough, makes the best of a bad situation, and chooses to wait rather than do what goes against the grain. Not always, but as a rule. Some dogs are dirtier than others. But I've had adults who would howl in the agony of a disordered stomach all night rather than dirty their kennel. Dogs, like human beings, can be taught a great deal of self-control, far more than people realize. They can be taught to control their physical impulses, but the lesson should come from within. Self-control in a dog is the paramount sign of canine civilization.

Now that I have my puppy clean in her kennel through being tied up—this lesson should bear fruit in less than a week—I let her loose one night, and the chances are that the kennel will be as clean as usual in the morning. She has formed a new habit, that of self-control during the time she is confined. If she isn't clean, I make her feel ashamed by pointing out what she's done with a scolding. She'll understand.

In the meantime, she has been coming into the house at various short times during the day. But not in the same way that yours runs about enjoying himself, jumping on the furniture, tearing the curtains and your slippers, making pools now and then on the carpet, and wolfing titbits at meals. Heaven forbid! My puppy comes in on a lead, and as soon as I settle in any room, is given some special place or corner on the floor, plus her own rug or bed, which afterwards she always occupies. She is tied up, and has no alternative but to lie quietly on her bed. Dogs on the furniture are a sign of human ignorance. No whining is allowed, but you'll remember she was cured of noise and howling a long time ago in the kennel. When I consider she has been long enough inside, or if she is growing fidgety, I take her out, and either bring her in again for a further spell, or put her back in the kennel. It all depends what I'm doing. Training a puppy is a full-time job in the process, and if you haven't time or opportunity to do it properly, then put your puppy away until you have. Never be sloppy or careless about training. Either do it properly or not at all. Nothing else will serve, and that is one reason why an outside kennel is so useful.

When my puppy comes into the dining-room for meals, she must go to her corner and *stay there*. Here again I find the lead valuable during these first lessons. After the meal is over, and if the puppy has behaved quietly and well, she is given a little bit of meat or food I've saved for her. This is necessary if I'm training for any special purpose, such as sitting up, or asking for food with a bark.

Actually coming into the house for the night is the final lesson, in which all the previous experiences play their part. The puppy has her bed in a corner of the room, and is tied up rather shortly, even though she has been clean in her kennel during the previous fortnight or so. There's hardly a chance of her doing wrong on this night. If my training has been any good at all, the puppy won't disappoint me; and when I go down early in my dressing-gown to let her out in the morning, I feel satisfied that nearly all the troubles are over. It is now a matter of gradually leaving off the lead as the puppy grows used to her life, habits, and surroundings. The result is a well-behaved house-dog, quiet, unobtrusive, and no bother to anyone. Automatically she finds her own place in any room and stays there. By degrees, of course, discipline can be relaxed, but it's better to be firm in the beginning than to try to give a belated training. When I take her to other people's houses, she knows how to behave as a guest should, and will obediently settle herself anywhere I put her, and never go begging at meals.

The chief advantage of this particular method is that it minimizes all risk of wrong-doing and actual dirt in the house. I've had one or two puppies who, in fact, have never committed a crime in the house at all. And that's how it should be. In other lines of training you sometimes want a dog to commit a fault in order to correct it, but this doesn't apply here at all.

Some Early Hints

Let's see what your dog is like at the same age. Bless his soul, he's full of spirits, and as soon as you open the door, he bounces in, muddy, wet, and delighted with himself. After leaving sundry streaks of mud by jumping up at everyone present, he leaps on the sofa, runs up and down a few times, and then scrapes a cushion into a comfortable position for his siesta. Unfortunately the siesta doesn't last very long, so he leaves the sofa, and patters endlessly round the room, making friends with people, wanting attention, tearing at trousers or skirts, and doing just what his dear little fancy dictates.

And meals. I don't like your puppy at meals, but it's not really his fault. You've encouraged him. You haven't? You don't? Then why give him something every time he leaps up and down beside you? Because it keeps him quiet? Don't you realize that because he receives some tasty bit as a result of his jumping, he does it all the more? Not only to you, unfortunately, but to everyone present. It's all very fatal to your dog's health and manners.

A word might be said here about this jumping-up habit, in which all puppies indulge if not corrected. They start as soon as they can crawl by nibbling at your shoelaces. *You* mightn't stop them, but I do. Give a sharp little kick whenever they start, and that'll soon stop the habit. Later they crawl up your legs and tear with catlike claws. As soon as you feel them doing this, bend down and give a quick tap on the nose. In fact, always discourage any tendency to leave the horizontal. Still later, the large and boisterous puppy leaps up with his straggling forepaws. This can be still more easily cured by a really hard smack on the nose as it appears. The boisterous puppy won't mind or take offence, and you'll be relieved of an annoying habit. So will your friends and visitors, which is more important.

We decided in the beginning what careers our respective puppies were going to have, but because yours is a housedog, there's no reason why he shouldn't be useful, or have his brain developed. Training begins as soon as you get your puppy—no later. You see, there are so many things a small puppy considers an amusing game, whereas actually you are planting seeds of future work.

There are trainers who wouldn't dream of starting an education until a dog is at least six months old. Until that time he lives the ordinary life of a kennel dog, which means his brain and intellectual capacities aren't keeping pace with his physical growth. And it's far more difficult to take out a raw six or eight months' puppy to train than one which has been gently educated since it was six weeks old.

Nosework can be encouraged from the beginning, and as the nose is one of the most important assets a dog possesses, it should be continually employed in various ways. Once a day you might drag a small, tasty piece of raw liver a yard or two, or perhaps in a circle in longish grass, and take the puppy to the place. He'll sniff about and find it, and during the time he's busy looking for the thing that is smelling so good, you tell him to seek, or whatever word you intend using permanently. Later, as he grows clever at finding this, you can vary the distances and places. And later still, throw the liver when he's not looking and then tell him to seek. After gazing at you for a minute, he'll suddenly realize what you mean, and go off, busily searching. You'll be surprised at the progress the puppy makes at this game, and how much you'll both enjoy it. Remember, though, that the seeking and eating game mustn't be confused with the retrieving game, even though there are many similar points between the two, and they should both start at the same time, as young as possible.

Another good method of making your puppy use his nose is to take him out, and when he's busy at some distance from you, you slip away and hide, preferably where you can watch him. As a rule he'll come back to where you should have been, then sniff round until he follows your line. A little later you get someone of whom he isn't particularly fond to hold him on a lead. Walk away in some definite direction, while he's watching. Let the assistant put a hand over his eyes after he has seen you start, so that you can get out of sight and hide, when the puppy can be released.

43

And when eventually he does find you, make a great fuss over him. This is a very childish start of a most useful accomplishment, and can be developed and varied *ad infinitum*.

Chapter 4

EARLY DISCIPLINE

Collar and Lead

Some puppies are angels to train to the collar and lead; the majority are just the opposite. I'll tell you first how I've seen you do this branch of training, and then how I do it myself.

You decide your naughty puppy must really learn to go on a lead. He gets so obstinate sometimes, and won't come back when you call him. Besides, it's not always convenient to have him loose everywhere. So you buy a lovely new stiff collar, and a lead which is frequently too light, or else a chain heavy enough to hold a Great Dane. The puppy is invested with his new collar, and with many misgivings, the lead attached. Immediately he feels any strain on his neck, there's a terrible to-do. Howls, screams, and struggles. You try to quieten him, and perhaps drag him a few steps. More screams of protest, until you get red in the face and think you must be committing some horrible crime. Poor little thing! Take the lead off at once. He doesn't like it. And as soon as the lead is removed the puppy, apart from scratching at his neck, is comparatively happy. This painful process goes on day after day, a long drawn out agony for all concerned. And when finally you imagine you've trained your puppy to the lead, I see him walking in front of you, pulling

45

with a strong, steady pull, while you proudly hold on with a firm grip and triumphant face. All his life your dog pulls you along. I meet you everywhere, especially in towns. If he sees a particularly tempting lamp-post, this taut tandem must rush thitherwards, and the party must wait until the dear thing has investigated. Well, well!

Now lead-training might start at the age of two months, or perhaps a little later. Personally I've used two methods with success, but the more recently devised has proved the most useful, as it constitutes a sort of two-in-one lesson. The first method is like extracting a tooth, a painful process, but rapidly over. It is of course only a start, but I believe in getting rid of the cruder necessities as quickly as possible. It is really the first time the puppy finds her will thwarted, and the noise made is more of a protest in temper than a feeling of pain. I wait for her to do something wrong, perhaps not coming when she's called to the kennel, and this is the best moment to start. I put on a suitable collar—preferably one that slips tight—a light chain, and tie her firmly to a post or small tree, just leaving her there. As soon as she feels the tightening of the chain and collar, there's a frightful noise, but apart from saying 'Shut up' once or twice, I take no notice. The puppy strains and pulls, and maybe hurts her neck, but I do nothing about it except scold slightly for noise. You see, my puppy never finds that a noise gets her out of trouble, but rather the opposite. After a time—and it may be a long time—she becomes quiet; the struggle has been tiring to body and mind. When I hear that the noise is finished, I walk up and pat and talk to her. I don't unfasten the chain, but walk away, and if she starts whining or struggling again, I admonish and leave her until there's another silence. Finally there comes a time when she says nothing, but sits looking quietly after me, resigned at last to the restraint. Then, and only then, I let her loose, removing both

46

collar and chain, and we enjoy a good game. The next day, or better, the next time there's any disobedience, the same process is repeated, and in a very short time the puppy realizes that cries and struggles don't pay, but silence and good behaviour do. Some breeds are far worse than others; so are some individuals. Some behave like wild animals, others like lambs. Needless to say, the reason for the chain in preference to a leather lead is that the latter may be soon bitten through when the puppy is left alone. Alsatians, owing to so much hereditary obedience work and control, are the easiest of all to train to the collar and lead. I've had a good many puppies which hardly required any training at all, and one marvellous three-months child walked behind me wearing a lead for the first time in the middle of a crowded shopping town.

This rapid method of preliminary lead training only resulted after many years' experience of puppies. I used to be like you, and tried to do it gently. But it's only a waste of time, and the results are just the same in the end, without any sacrifice of character, and a great saving of time and trouble. I shall now try to tell you about my second and most successful method.

For several weeks my puppy comes into her kennel when called. She does this because she wants to be with me, not at first realizing that the particular call means confinement. And of course the day comes when she either wakes up to this fact, or is enjoying herself too well to want to go into the kennel. I give her plenty of chance by calling her several times. She stands and looks at me, and then goes on with what she's doing or moves away. I give her another chance, and that failing, I leave her and go for my training-rope. This rope is a combination of lightness and strength, about the length of a good clothes-line, and has a strong swivel hook at one end, to which a slip-collar is attached. The puppy still moves away, and knows already she has done something wrong by my own silence. And this is where the two-in-one lesson comes in, since it teaches the puppy to come when called, and the feel of the lead straining on her neck. Best of all, this rather disagreeable experience takes place after she has done wrong.

I catch her by walking silently after her till she stops. It is more of a stroll than a walk, and I shall go on longer than she. You must never wildly chase a dog or puppy by running. They'll only laugh at you, and no wonder. With a hot pursuit they realize something is definitely wrong, but a gentle stroll makes them start thinking. When I catch up, the collar is slipped on, and if we are now far from the kennel I carry the puppy to the right distance for my lesson. Leaving her there, I take the extreme end of the rope to the kennel door, and call the puppy in. She may of course come immediately, in which case I praise her, and leave the lesson for another and more suitable time. But she'll probably sit on her haunches or go the other way. I call again, giving a sharp pull on the rope. This causes surprise. She can't understand why she comes willy-nilly nearer when she quite intended to go the other way. This is repeated until, very unwillingly, she reaches me, and is firmly thrust in. But we don't finish at that. The lesson has hardly begun. I take her out again and put her in the same position. The process is a repetition. I go on doing this until, at the extreme end of the rope, I call, and the puppy starts coming in of her own accord. This is a good step. We are both rather weary by this time, but I must go on, and so must the lesson. It becomes almost mechanical. Towards the end the puppy comes in on a slack rope, and is accordingly praised. Finally I take the rope off altogether, call with perfect results, and we have a stupendous celebration over the success of the lesson. It can be repeated whenever necessary later on.

When I put an ordinary lead on my puppy, she'll hardly notice it, because she knows that the strain on the collar means she must come. So I consider this the best method of all, and now my growing litters are trained in this way with quite surprising results. If anyone looks after them while I'm away, they are always astounded to see the puppies trotting in quite obediently when called.

Heel and Sit

The more advanced lead-training should be a three-in-one lesson. I've already pointed how ridiculous it is to be firmly towed along by your headstrong dog, going where he goes and stopping when he stops. He has a continual strain on his throat muscles, which presumably harden like the mouth of a cart-horse, and you have a considerable strain to hold the end of the lead. It's quite unnecessary. This is partly the result of your gentle training in the beginning. Your dog has never struggled against the impossible—an unyielding fence or chain. He knows if he pulls hard enough something will give. That's just what you mustn't let him think. If anything has to give, it's the dog.

Both my preliminary methods prove to the puppy that there's not only something stronger, but a force quite impossible to contend with. So my second set of lessons should be more successful than yours.

The three lessons learnt in the next stage are walking with a slack lead, keeping in to heel, and sitting. If your dog does these things satisfactorily he's a joy to take out, instead of a nuisance and a curse. There's no better example of perfect heel-work than that exacted in the Alsatian obedience tests, but you want to bring this into practical life as well as in the ring. Incidentally, I once owned a wonderful obedience-working bitch who, in the ring, would hardly lose a mark for her heel-work, but who forgot all about it when out for a walk! In all fairness to myself I must say I hadn't trained her, and in the life she had led previously there hadn't been much need for keeping in to heel. All gun-dogs must learn this early lesson, and for them it's one of the important necessities.

So we'll assume I'm taking my puppy out seriously on a lead for the first time. I choose a rather quiet, spacious place, such as a large field. I use a choke collar, one that tightens at a pull, as it works much quicker and is more effective. I place the puppy on my left-hand side and attach the lead. Bending down, with the left hand I push her hindquarters to the ground, and lifting her chin with the right, I say 'Sit'. Until she has remained quietly in this position for a few seconds, I don't move. Then, with my left hand rather low down on the lead, I walk forward, saying, 'Heel'. The puppy will probably try to bound on in front, and is pulled back very sharply with the left hand, and again brought into the correct position before starting off. Now I may have a puppy who is inclined to keep ahead, or it may be one who lags behind. Both can be corrected by a sharp pull, so sharp that the lead is slack before tightening again. Let me say once and for all that a steady pull on the puppy's collar is *no use at all* in lead-training. The pull must be something of a wrench, relief coming immediately she regains the correct position, and a slack lead. It's the contrast that makes this training a success. When the puppy goes wrong, her neck is jerked, but when she's right, she feels no strain at all. Gradually she realizes that in one special position—the correct one —there is no sudden pull, and everything is comfortable. This is really an unconscious conclusion, but it always comes eventually. I walk about, always keeping the puppy by my left leg, stopping occasionally, when she must instantly sit until I move on again. This may sound difficult, but in reality is quite easy to put into practice, whether a slow puppy must be jerked up, or a forward one pulled back.

In a very obstinate case of 'forwardness' I take a switch or small stick in my right hand, and tap the puppy's nose whenever it appears beyond its allotted place. This is always successful. Remember, the allotted place is neither behind nor before you: the dog's head should be beside your left leg.

This heel-training, which becomes more complicated later on, must not be attempted before the puppy has had some experience with the lead. It's the second stage, not the first. Here again most Alsatians are almost miraculous in their aptitude, and I've taken out puppies who behave as though they've done it all their lives instead of for the first time. A great example of inherited instinct.

The first day of this mustn't last long, or the puppy becomes bored and tired, an undesirable state in training. Ten minutes or a quarter of an hour is quite long enough, after which you give all freedom, and play with the puppy before putting it away. It's advisable to give a certain time every day to this particular lesson, as it is extremely practical and useful. Vary the places, vary the turns, and the pace. Be sure the puppy always keeps his place, and sits as soon as you stop, even though you may go round in a small circle, or stop for five minutes. You'll be amazed at the rapid results. You'll find that very soon he sits as soon as you stop, without being told, and that he keeps his place almost like a machine. Take him among people and crowds; let the same words serve, and the same actions. You'll be well on the way to having a useful dog, one that is never a bother, who comes to heel or sits by you on command.

Don't try it without the lead for a considerable time. Eventually of course he'll do it all without one, but you must first induce an invariable habit, so that it comes automatically. In this way you are laying the foundations of a perfectly behaved dog, and—in the case of my puppy—a steady gun-dog. Always reward good behaviour with your voice and caresses. Dogs understand and appreciate this a good deal more than people imagine, so much so that a slight inflexion in the voice can make all the difference.

Early Walks

From now on, we are taking our puppies for walks, you n your way, I in mine. You are walking partly for your own pleasure, partly as a duty, and partly because it's rather fun to take out a dog. I meet you in this stage, your puppy bounding about where and how he likes. You gaze at the scenery or the trees while he chases someone else's chickens, and when at last you see him ambling after the portly old rooster which he can never just catch, you scream with laughter because he looks so amusing, bless his little heart. Or he may do some ambling among the sheep, barking in a squeaky voice while they stand and look at him. You don't stop him, of course. The poor little thing is far too young to do any harm. When you walk along, your eyes elsewhere, your puppy just behind you, you never see him steal a few feet to one side and eat some filth. Belatedly you look behind, and think he's lagging. But when you get home you wonder if a rat has died under the floor, or *could* it be the dog's breath? You bet it could! Again, as you admire the view or chatter to your friend, the puppy rolls himself thoroughly in another lot of filth. This, when you discover it, makes you really roused. I've seen you beating him for it. But how did he know he shouldn't have indulged in an old hereditary custom? How could he tell for what reason the beating was given if you hadn't caught him in the act?

Then there's the running-away game, when I've seen you,

red-faced and quite angry, in hot pursuit of your strong-willed puppy, who only laughs as he runs faster. If and when you do catch him, his chastisement generally depends on the length of the race or the state of your temper. All of which is most regrettable.

Let me tell you this. Though you may be keeper, shepherd, or just an ordinary person, when you take your dogs or puppies for a walk, it's for *their* benefit and amusement and training, not yours. If you want to admire views or gossip with your friends, leave the untrained dogs behind. Because, until you've trained yourself, you can't do several things at once.

As soon as the lead starts in earnest, by the method I described last, I am busy practising the lessons, so that my puppy is already fairly obedient when eventually she goes for walks. At first I take the trouble to carry the training-rope until I see perfect results when I call the puppy in to heel. After all, I suppose answering a call is the first order a dog should obey, not, mark you, because he wants to be with you of his own free will, but because you've told him you want him.

I shall, however, make a few remarks about the period immediately preceding the lead business, which also apply to the times your puppy is running free when you let him off the lead. Never forget you are walking for the dog's sake, not your own. You'd find, if you strolled with a keeper who has a spaniel, retriever, or setter, that, although he's talking to you quite intelligently, he never looks away from his dog for long, and invariably knows what he's doing and where he is. You must be like that when your puppy goes with you for walks. It's so easy to correct faults before they happen, or the moment they take place, and is worth ten punishments *after* the deed is done.

Imagine my puppy is very small, and can follow a little

way across the field where I take her. She is behind me as I walk along. I notice some cow dung or sheep droppings—inevitable temptation to puppies, and the surest way to develop worms. Slowly I go towards this, step over it, at the same time turning round to watch the puppy. She stops, attracted by the smell, and just as I see she's going to try a sample, I bend down with the sort of vocal corrective noise reserved for these occasions, and give her a sharp smack. This must all be repeated several times, with all sorts of tempting bait, and is an example of trying to make the dog do wrong in order that you may put it right. With this also, you'll be surprised at the quick results. In my own case it's generally a litter of puppies, and I find it so successful that later I can make any of them drop even a bone when I make the particular noise, which sounds like a gruff, drawn-out Ah-h-h. Naturally the smack which must at first be associated with the voice can soon be dispensed with. The effect is just the same.

So you see, even these apparently trifling details are worth a good deal of attention, and are in themselves an early training for you to be fit to educate your dog later. You come to a state when, quite unconsciously, you watch your dog all the time you may be busy with something else. That third eye is developed, the vigilant, interested eye that must miss no detail. Notice if your puppy relieves all his physical needs on the walk. See what reaction there is to a rabbit's scent or that of a pheasant, even in quite early days. If a bird flies across the path, is he observant and quick, or slow and apparently blind?

Meanwhile, play games with him, be jolly, join in his primitive ideas of fun, so long as they aren't definitely mischievous. When, later, he shows signs of chasing live things, you can make the same disapproving noises that you produced over the question of his bad taste. And incidentally, when your puppy chases, it's the only justified occasion when you can run after him in what I called hot pursuit, but you'll have a whip in your hand when you do. Always, without exception, discourage the chasing tendency from the beginning. I shall illustrate this later when I talk about his relationship with other animals.

Chapter 5

CIVILIZING A PUPPY

~~~

Self-help

Happily dogs, like people, differ enormously in personality, character, and temperament. It's the study of individual personality and reaction that makes training so interesting, and precludes the danger of any mechanical process.

Many puppies, especially of the larger breeds, hesitate to go up or down stairs, in spite of all persuasion. This difficulty can be overcome in half an hour if you go the right way about it. You mustn't give any help, or try to drag the puppy up by his lead, and, instead of standing at the top or bottom, beseeching with your best cajolery, just take the puppy bodily and dump him right in the middle of the staircase. Then go either up or down—better up—and call. But don't hang about and waste time. Call once or twice and walk away. The puppy is left to his own devices, and has no alternative but to help himself, which he does eventually in a somewhat clumsy and very noisy fashion. This procedure should be repeated several times in succession, until the puppy is quite comfortable about it, and will follow without hesitation. This overcoming of difficulties without human aid is one of the secrets of successful training. A self-taught experience is more valuable than any amount of orders. It makes the dog use his brain; it makes him think. With what pleasure later on you see your dog performing some difficult achievement, thinking it out, and using the brain you helped to develop by making him work independently!

Another excellent chance comes for this sort of practice when the puppy is out for walks. No matter how small he is, you must look round for some obstacle—a little stream, a fence, a ditch—something which you can judge he can physically overcome, but might hesitate over because it's strange to him. You walk through, across, or over it, and cast a glance backwards to see what happens, though still walking on and calling his name. He stops, looks at the obstacle, and after running up and down once or twice, begins to whimper. You keep calling him, but walk slowly on all the time. If you stop, he'll think you're coming back to lift him out of the difficulty and won't try himself. He shrieks, howls, and runs from one side to the other in a frenzy. Sooner or later he grows calmer, summons all his small courage, and finds the easiest way over or through the obstacle. He may flounder in a stream, or struggle for a moment in a ditch. He may have to push through a gap in a thorn hedge, or climb over a bank. But in the end he comes, a little galloping object, full of pride and pleasure at having overcome the trouble to be with you again. You both have a joyous celebration over this, and you'll be surprised how quickly he surmounts the next obstacle.

This sort of preliminary training applies to all breeds, whether Pekingese or mastiffs, Poms or Great Danes. The difficulties can be varied according to the size of the dog, but the principle is the same. It always surprises and faintly shocks me to see you lifting your dear little puppy over this and that, helping him here and there, when he can perfectly well help himself. Anyone might think he was a child, and heaven forbid that dogs should be as helpless and dependent as children, though they have the same type of brain. Actually of course, children are far more pampered over these things than your puppy. It might be better for them if sometimes they were treated in a similar way.

Because later you are going to deprive the dog of much of his independent spirit and free will, you should always encourage the sort of independence that training can't interfere with, and which will be an asset in subsequent work. There are times—many times—when the most highly trained dog must think for himself, though this independent thought follows an order or command. Again the retriever can be used as an example. He has been told to fetch a wounded bird. His handler doesn't know any more than he where the bird is, or how far it may have gone, though both saw it fall. And if he is a well-trained and experienced dog, the handler will be wise to let him work out the problem in his own way. Sometimes the results are an extraordinary revelation of common sense and deduction. The experienced dog knows that the bird will run on somewhere until he finds, if possible, a thick place in which to hide. If the line seems to lead to a bramble bush or a dense hedge, the dog will frequently take a short cut to these hiding-places, just as an old spaniel knows exactly the sort of cover where game sits, and will go out of his way to make for it.

This is independent action. The dog is released to work on his own, his orders merely send him away, and he must do the rest. Of course, when he's at a loss, and can't think of any further move, his handler must help and suggest. When you start training dogs for any performance that involves this independent action in finding hidden objects, you are far too inclined to get in the way in an unnecessary desire to help. But you discover eventually that the dog's nose is far more reliable than your own imagination, and when he says the thing is in one direction, you'd be wise to listen to that advice, even though you thought it was the opposite.

Independence produces thought, but the ideal combination of handler and dog, teacher and pupil, is a mixture of this independence, training, and control. You tell me *your* dog is independent. I can see that. He does exactly as he likes, without proper correction. His thoughts and actions are employed entirely to suit *him*, not you. Whereas you should be using every ounce of your skill in making him think for *your* benefit, not his. You'd both be happier with the result. Life would be much more fun, and infinitely more interesting.

Speaking or Sitting Up

As you rear and bring up your puppy, to you he's just a dog. Just a dog, like every other puppy. Perhaps you don't notice that he has peculiarities and a personality of his own. But he has, all the same, and it would be as well to give the matter a little attention. Any natural habits that seem to be useful should be encouraged. Always study the individual dog and his instinctive actions, and make full use of every opportunity. Take feeding, for instance.

When I feed, which always takes place at the same times every day if possible, I don't just put down the bowl and not take any more interest. For one thing, the way the dog eats her meal is an indication of the state of health and appetite. She dances about in expectation of the food, and perhaps makes a slight squeak. If she's a small dog I should teach her to sit up before receiving food, but if a member of a larger breed, I train her to 'speak'. On the whole, the former is the easier lesson, at least in results, but if desired both can be combined with the old 'trust and paid for' trick which our grandparents used to find so intriguing. Actually it's not a

59

bad idea, because it teaches control and has a good effect on the dog's character. In any case, no puppy should be allowed to dash in the moment the food is put on the ground. If you were teaching him nothing else, you should make him pause. You don't let your child snatch wildly at everything he sees as soon as he reaches the table, so why the puppy?

It's hardly necessary to detail here the easy lesson of sitting up and begging. (Yes, I know you have taught your dog to do this: he does nothing else when there's food about.) But there are several ways, and this, like almost every other detail of training, should be started as young as possible, as soon, in fact, as the puppy can sit comfortably on her haunches. I find the easiest method is to pick out a nice bit of meat from the rest, putting the bowl aside for the moment, and then hold the piece just out of reach of the puppy's nose. As she raises her head, I lift her chest and tell her to sit up at the same time. Jumping after the bait must be firmly discouraged, as it leads to nothing, and the puppy must never be given her choice bit until she is in the proper position. It may help to move her so that she has her back supported by a wall. The chief thing to remember is to keep the hind-legs in a sitting position, and not let her dance about. I wait until she is steady, then lower the meat until she can take it. At this moment she will be almost balanced independently in the desired position. The lesson can be repeated immediately with another bit, and then finally I hold the bowl, making her sit up again before putting it down in front of her. The sitting-up lesson is one that can be practised several times during the day, and the puppy is only too willing to learn, as the trick brings an edible reward. When she has her bone, she must sit up for that too. In a comparatively short time she will stay in the position without help, and later on will go up on her own as soon as she sees the food. The command must of course be given every time, so that she knows what it means, and will eventually obey whether there is food or not.

You may argue that there's no point in making a dog look ridiculous by begging, but you see, it's a lesson in discipline, it's an easy preliminary both for you and the puppy to the later more practical accomplishments. Anyway, see if it feels ridiculous when yours sits up for the first time by himself! You'll find yourself as proud as a mother when her child first staggers across the floor on his wobbly legs.

Recently, and at first unintentionally, I taught one of my young bitches to balance herself almost indefinitely on her hind-legs, just as a human being stands up. This was her own alternative to the proper sitting up, which originally she could do quite well. As she grew larger, she found it easier to stand instead of sit on her hind-legs. This I encouraged, and now she is almost remarkable in the balancing feat, which is always difficult for a dog, but which she can keep up for a considerable time with hardly a shift of her feet. It is a further development of this that reproduces the dog who walks right across the circus ring on his hind-legs.

Asking audibly for food is a more useful item in the training list than it may appear, and if I had the time I should teach all my puppies and dogs this trick. It really means making the dog bark on command, which is indispensable to the complicated training of guarding an object, a place, or a car. In any case it's useful to be able to order your dog to bark when you wish.

This is definitely to be learnt at the youngest age possible, and the older the puppy, the more difficult it is to teach. I start almost as soon as she begins to eat regular meals. Though the actual method of teaching is simpler than the previous trick, the result generally takes much longer to arrive, and a good deal of time and patience will have to be used. It varies with the amount of greed in the individual dogs. Puppies who love their food are quicker to learn than those who just don't mind whether they eat or not. That's why the training must be started young, before the growing appetite has given way to maturer finickings.

I try to get my puppy thoroughly hungry, and then let her have a good-smell at the food-bowl. After that, the proceeding merely consists of standing in front of her with the bowl, and saying 'Speak!' She dances about, says nothing, jumps up and down, and shows every sign of impatience except by the desired sound. Sometimes to vary the monotony I hold the bowl nearer for her to have another smell. After a bit she thinks that this is merely another of my eccentricities, and decides to wait until I've regained my senses. Being a sensible puppy who has already some knowledge of her curious handler, she sits down patiently to wait. You see, up to now any noise has been ruthlessly suppressed, so it's the last thing that occurs to her. You can't have it every way, and if the previous lessons of silence have been effective, it will generally take longer to produce a good healthy bark.

If the puppy refuses altogether to make a sound, she must still go hungry. I take the food away, and generally put her in the kennel for half an hour or so, after which the proceedings start all over again. Possibly this second attempt will produce the desired result, even if she only gives a squeak of impatience. That's enough to start with, and the moment I hear this squeak, the bowl is put down, the puppy praised and patted. The chief point is perseverance and firmness. You mustn't be in a hurry, or so occupied that you can't afford the time to keep coming back to try. Above all, the food must be withheld until a sound arrives, even though it means leaving her hungry for several hours. It goes on every day for every meal, and at last the puppy will prick up her ears, look intelligent, and on the command to speak, will let out a really good bark.

There are other ways of making an older dog speak to order, but they sometimes involve hurting him in some way until he protests vocally, which is, in my opinion, a mistake, and doesn't tend to maintain a good relationship between dog and handler. The dog you are training should always rely on you, and therefore knows he doesn't get hurt unless he really deserves it. By far the quickest method to achieve the speak is to make the puppy bark before being let out of the kennel, which most of them are only too willing to do. But this is in direct opposition to the silence-in-the-kennel rule, and has nothing to commend it. Naturally, if the puppy were freed every time he barked, he'd do it all day long.

In many books and hints on training, the giving of titbits as rewards for good performances is advocated. I think this is a terrible mistake, and can never understand why anyone should either give the advice or follow it. Your dog should obey orders and work with you, not for the reward that satisfies his greed, but because it's his job, and because he enjoys having his brain usefully occupied. Would you think of rewarding a child by means of his stomach every time he behaved well? If you would, then you haven't learnt the elements of training, whether of dogs or children. Just as a child should have a better motive for his good actions than food, so should your puppy. Perhaps people have found they get better results by the reward system, but if I couldn't train my dogs without titbits, I should never try again.

No, the only time this is justified is by using food as the means to a trick generally connected with food, such as begging or speaking. Even then, a greedy dog may be over anxious to perform at all sorts of times later on if he thinks he'll get something to eat by so doing. This can be checked, however, and the dog shown that no results ensue unless he performs only as the result of a command.

The Car

It may seem as though you and your puppy will have a good deal of fully occupied time during this bringing up business. It may seem as if he has too much to learn at once, but this is not so. All these youthful lessons more or less intertwine, and are connected with each other. They fit in with the ordinary life you lead, except that you must be *dog*-conscious and not *un*conscious. That's why I advocate a kennel, anyway at first, so that you can always put the puppy away when you really haven't time to give him the attention he requires. Otherwise, when he's with you, you must keep an eye on what he does, if you want him to turn out a decent member of canine society. You have so many opportunities of training him all the time you are leading your own life, and it needn't really interfere with your home occupations at all. You'll be surprised to notice the unconscious sense developing in yourself, the sense which all real trainers attain, enabling them to walk and talk, to do this and that, but always keeping an eye on their dogs at the same time.

There are several places where you'll want to take your puppy, partly because you want him with you, and partly because there are times when you can't very well leave him behind. For instance, all modern dogs must learn to travel properly in a car. And when I say properly I mean properly. Let's consider the average dog, for instance. As soon as any car door is opened, he leaps in and up on a seat—it doesn't matter which seat. He jumps from the front to the back, or vice versa. He rubs his nose on the windows, leaving wet splodges, and claws at the upholstery while doing so. If anyone is unfortunate enough to have to sit behind, he lies all over them, covering them with hairs, and never keeps still for a second. If the window happens to be open, he strains his head out until his eyes water profusely, scratching the paint to do so. As soon as the door is opened at the end of the journey—or perhaps not at the end—he leaps out again, before anyone else has a chance to move. Above all, if he's the car-sick kind, he dribbles all over everything, eventually planting his unwelcome stomach contents anywhere and everywhere. No, I don't say every dog or puppy possesses all these faults, or half of them. I'm just combining the various faults in one dog as an easy way of enumerating them. I'm sure for instance, that if your dog likes to shove his head out of the window, he doesn't belong to the Car-sick Brethren. But you see what I mean, don't you? It's not civilized, not manners. You see, this sort of thing will never make your dog—or any dog—popular with people who don't care for them.

I like cars too much to enjoy having dogs in them at all, but if it's necessary, there are ways of doing it more or less decently. All my own dogs and puppies are car-trained. It's part of their education, a necessary but disagreeable part. I admit I'm not one of those people who find it indispensable to take my dog everywhere I go. Maybe I see quite enough of them at home! I can't really see why anyone does such a thing for pleasure, because the dog often has to sit, bored to death, in the car, while the owner is enjoying himself else-where, or doing the family shopping. And who wants a dog shopping? Sometimes he's useful as a guard, if you leave your car anywhere. But I can remember an occasion when I left two large Alsatians in my car one night outside a cinema, thinking no one would dare to open the door or go near it. To my surprise I came out to find the commission-aire with the door open, pushing the car farther up the rank, and two 'fierce' Alsatians calmly lying down, watching him with smiles and wagging tails. That was the doubtful penalty of keeping sweet-tempered Alsatians!

To return to car-training. It's better to wait until the puppy is several months old, and therefore having fewer meals, before attempting to take him in a car. You can, of course, start quite young, provided you have a good box with plenty of bedding, and preferably an empty puppy. But the difference between the clean, jolly dog that went in and the bedraggled, nasty object that comes out will perhaps give you a shock, and postpone this amusement till later on.

Some dogs seem to be car-sick all their lives, and others soon get over it, or are never sick at all. I think also that certain breeds are more inclined to suffer than others. I am convinced, however, that 90 per cent of dogs can be cured permanently, if only they were taken out often enough. It's largely a matter of practice. I find that even an older dog who was quite proof against car-sickness, but who hasn't been out for some time, occasionally has lapses. I know of men in the Navy who say they are always ill when they first go out after a long leave, and who have to become re-acclimatized.

The best and quickest cure of all is a long journey, involving many hundreds of miles, and perhaps several days. Two setters once travelled down from Scotland to Devonshire in this way. Neither was car-trained or used to travelling in this manner. Thank Heaven it was a two-seater, and they occupied the dickey at the back! The journey took three days. The first they spent in being continually sick, but on the last two were quite happy, as though they'd been in a car all their lives. Naturally this method would be rather expensive, and not very practicable to the average person. But it works even with quite small puppies, and shows, I think, that it's a matter of being accustomed to the movement.

I'll imagine now that I'm going to start my puppy on her car-training. She's four months old, and therefore accustomed to the collar and lead, to sitting quietly where put, and has only two meals a day. First of all I lay a few sacks on the floor in the back of the car. Then I open the door, holding the puppy beside me on the lead. She is unwilling to climb in, so I find the best way is to get in myself, and gently pull her over the step. Why don't people always train their dogs to go on the floor instead of the seats? It's just as comfortable, especially if they have their own rug, and it does save so much dirt and trouble. Besides, the dog should never be allowed on the furniture in the house; why therefore on the car seat? Having manœuvred my puppy in, nicely placed on the sacks, I tie her up rather shortly to a seat-support or something convenient behind the front seats, telling her to sit. Then we start off, and if possible this first journey must be short, and punctuated with frequent stops. If the puppy looks like being sick, or is dribbling excessively, I take her out and give her a little run. Of course she may be quite happy, in which case I keep going on, rather slowly. It's best to avoid any chances of her being sick by this short journey method, because she can be educated to the car motion by degrees, and so become proof in a short time. Later on the sacks can be dispensed with, and also the lead, once the puppy has learnt to lie on the floor, and never attempts to go anywhere else. It becomes an automatic habit, and as she has never jumped on the seat at all, she'll never want to. Imagine what trouble this saves. No smeared windows, no scratched paint, or muddy seat-coverings. No chances of jumping from the back to the front seat, or out of the windows. All the time the puppy is quite comfortable. In an open car this prevents any tendency to jumping out when the car is stationary.

It's no use your telling me your puppy just won't keep on the floor. I don't care whether it's an old dog or a young one, it can be trained just the same. Tie him up so that he *can't* jump on the seat for a few journeys, and you'll find he'll stay there afterwards. Don't give up, smilingly and indulgently saying dogs will be dogs. Dogs are what you make them, no more and no less.

Another point about car-training. Never let the dog get in or out of the car except by command. There's nothing more trying than a dog who makes a dash for the door as soon as it's opened. You can stop this by a little practice at home. It'll save you endless bother. Sit the dog, open the car door, keep the dog sitting for a few seconds—the longer the better. Then give the order 'Get in', and see he goes to his correct place. Shut the door, open it again, telling the dog to sit, and if necessary keeping him back in position with your hand. Step back and call him out after a minute or so. This will want some practice before it becomes perfect, but it's well worth it. Concentrate especially on opening the door when the dog is inside. If he's very determined about coming out in a hurry, shut the door quickly on him as he comes. You'll find you'll be more popular if you have a dog who behaves decently, not only in your own car, but in other people's.

Chapter 6

FURTHER DISCIPLINE

The Sit

The primary essential of any dog's training is to sit properly, which means staying or resting in one place until released. It comes into nearly everything the dog learns later, and is incorporated in every working dog's schedule. The collie, spaniel, setter, and retriever must drop on command. In fact no dog can be controlled properly unless or until this is thoroughly instilled. In its further more complicated stages it's one of the most useful of the dog's accomplishments.

Perhaps you think you've trained *your* dog to sit when he's told. Forgive me, but you've done nothing of the sort. You vaguely fling him an off-hand command to sit or lie down, and if he feels like it, he does so; if not, he runs about just the same as before. Now I don't want to repeat myself too often, but I must make this clear. When you give an order, it must be obeyed, always, without exception. And if you're too busy to see it carried out, then put it off altogether until later on.

The sit lesson takes some considerable time and trouble to teach in the beginning, but you can start when you have half an hour to spare. The puppy should be over three months old, unless the lesson has been already begun by the heel-sit-lead performance, which, in my experience, is the best start of all, as the puppy already knows what 'Sit' means before regular practice begins.

In obedience tests they draw a sharp line between sitting and lying down. For all practical purposes this is quite unnecessary, and real working dogs don't have to bother with these finicking details. When I want my dog to stay in one place I don't really care if she stands on her head, sits on her tail, or lies on her back, so long as she knows I want her to stay there until told to do otherwise. This applies to gunwork, and the chief reason I insist on a sitting or lying position to start with is to emphasize that the dog must stay there, perhaps for some considerable time. Similarly a young setter or spaniel is made to drop to a shot or rising game. As they grow older and more experienced, they may not take the trouble to go right down, but that doesn't matter as long as they are firm and steady and know what is required.

As I've already taught my puppy to sit when she walks and stops beside me, she knows the word and what it means. Which makes things a little easier for the first lesson. I take her out on the lead and walk round as usual, the puppy on my left. When I stop, she sits, perhaps automatically by now. I hold her in this position, and turn round to face her, so that she is sitting in front of me. Putting my hand under her jaw, I command, 'Sit', in a firm voice, and let the lead drop, at the same time taking away my hand. She sits beautifully, and I let her do so for several minutes: any attempt at moving away or jumping up is strongly discouraged by repeating the command, and keeping her in position by hand. If I find this works perfectly the first time, I move away a yard or two, by stepping slowly backwards, still repeating the command. Now with my own dogs I always raise the right hand as a signal to sit or drop. This is indispensable out shooting, when as little noise as possible must be made. But I shall talk about signs later. There's no special need for you to use a signal in addition to your voice, unless you intend going on with me to more complicated performances. When I move backwards, my puppy thinks this means a continuation of the walk, and may follow. But if she's sensible, she understands she has been told to sit, and does so. Unless she's proved particularly brilliant up till now, I put off this moving until next time. When it takes place, and she tries to come after me, I go back quietly and keep her in the original position. The sitting lesson continues at intervals at all times of the day, indoors and out, and indeed at some time during every day of the dog's life.

But we'd better go back and see how you're getting on with your lesson. As your puppy is wilder, more bouncing, and less controlled than mine, you'll find it more difficult, and so will he. He hasn't learnt anything, and so starts from the very beginning. Right. Take him firmly under the throat, and hold him in front of you. Wait till he's finished trying to bounce up and down and play with you. Be serious, and let him know this isn't a game at all, but something more important. Put your left hand over his back and press his hindquarters down, forcibly, if necessary. Give the command 'Sit' repeatedly, and keep his chin up, because it's easier to keep down his hindquarters with the head up. Eventually you'll manage to get him sitting quietly. Hold him there for some time, always repeating the command. You'll probably have to go on with this very elementary lesson several times a day for several days, and when you see he understands how to sit quietly on command in front of you, then try moving backwards a step. If necessary, drive a peg into the ground, and tie him shortly to it, so that he can't follow you, and always return to him if he gets up or moves. It doesn't matter in the least if he lies down. I consider it a sign the lesson is learnt when my puppy settles

71

herself comfortably down, chin on paws, at the command of 'Sit'. It shows she realizes she must stay in the same place, and not move elsewhere.

With small, fidgety breeds, there's endless trouble to arrive at satisfactory results. You may have to put the puppy back twenty times in as many minutes. But the chief thing to remember here, as in all training, is to persevere until success comes—go on longer than the dog—tire him out if necessary—so long as you gain your point. And always, without fail, finish on success. Let the lesson end as soon as the puppy has done—and done well—what you wanted. This is of course the very elementary stage. The rest comes by degrees. You keep moving farther away, you make the puppy sit longer at a time, and so on.

Back and Recall

Eventually I train my growing puppy so that she sits in all circumstances and conditions when told to do so, and to the command of 'Sit' is added a new word. This is 'Back', which really means: 'Whatever happens you mustn't go forward or follow me.' I use this command later on when I want to leave my dog anywhere, and perhaps go out of sight myself. Or if I have any special job to do where a dog would be in the way, I first sit her, and then say, 'Back'. For instance, not long ago I found a sick-looking sheep among some rocks, and wanted to investigate. I had four dogs and two small puppies with me, and naturally didn't want them near the sheep. I put all the old dogs down, and told them to keep back; the puppies followed their example, and I was able to move the sheep into an easier position without it being frightened by the dogs.

If you put your puppy down and are able to leave him and go some distance away, start by walking in a circle round him, and always end by returning to the puppy. Keep him in his position for a moment, and then let him free to do as he likes. You see, if you go away, and after some time call him to you, it frequently makes him anticipate the call, and come bounding along at any minute. But if he knows he must wait till you come back, he remains patiently where he is. Increase the circle by degrees. Stroll for a second out of sight, but always be ready to go back to the puppy and scold him if he shows the slightest sign of rising. If by any chance he leaves the place where you put him, discovers his mistake, and lies or sits again somewhere else, always take him back, scolding, to the original position. Above all make sure his steadiness is complete at one stage before beginning another. Don't be in a hurry with the training; let every lesson sink well in.

After a time you'll find he'll sit anywhere on command. Try this when out for a walk, when he isn't thinking of anything special and is running gaily in front of you. Call or whistle to demand attention, and then give the command to sit. If your previous training has been thorough, he'll do so at once. If not, you must go up and put him in position. I know all this sounds like hard work, but you'll have overcome many difficulties when he obeys at last.

A little later still, make him sit, walk away as far as possible, turn round facing him, and after a few seconds, call him to you. He should come at full gallop, and when he arrives, make him sit in front of you. It gives a sort of neat finish to the recall, and in the case of a retriever or spaniel is most helpful, as that's more or less what he must do when he brings back the bird or rabbit.

Then try another variation. I assure you that if your previous training has been sound, and your judgment as to the time for this new experiment correct, it'll work on the very first occasion you try it. I've succeeded here with puppies

73

aged only eight weeks. Repeat the recall just described, only when your puppy is about half-way to you, suddenly shout 'Sit!' And he will, probably at once, which looks very effective, and makes you think you're really a trainer at last! Of course if you've used the raised hand in conjunction with your voice, it works much better, as the puppy sees rather than hears your command. If by any chance he doesn't drop at once, go towards him quickly, repeating the order, until he does. Then move back, and try it again. Keep him down for a few seconds and call him in to you, making him sit for a minute before you praise him. Never forget this latter. He loves it, and you can't give too much when the work has been good. But don't do this interrupted recall too often, or your puppy will never come in freely, but will always be waiting for the order to drop.

With my own puppy, since she must have a gun-dog's training, I invariably signal by hand. At first she obeys the voice, but later grows to learn and look for the signal which accompanies the vocal command. By the time she's six months old, she's always dropped by a sharp whistle—to gain attention—and a raised arm. This method has the advantage of being useful at a long distance, and seems to me neater and more efficient.

It's very useful to be able to make your dog sit or drop in all circumstances. Apart from the convenience of keeping him quiet and obedient in the house, it has its advantages in other people's houses, cars, and gardens. It's helpful if he shows signs of chasing live stock or anything else. You have noticed that all my lessons are so far connected with each other, and that if the puppy doesn't learn by one method, she does by another. The kennel, house-training, the car, the lead, and finally the definite lessons of advanced sitting are closely related, and each one of them tends to produce a decent, quietly behaved dog.

Naturally, when puppies are young, the lessons must be short and frequent. Try not to let your puppy become too bored. It may go against you next time. If you see signs of approaching boredom, hurriedly get your successful result, and leave it at that. On the other hand, don't leave it unless it *is* a result.

Further Discipline

All this training sounds very mechanical, rather as though you are trying to make your dog into an automaton. This, I'm afraid, must be so in the beginning, but as soon as the elementary lessons are learnt—and they take almost longer to explain than to do—the whole situation changes. You evolve a huge and varied repertoire in which the dog takes part, employing his brains, thought, and every sense he has. It's largely up to you to create the programme and vary the performances, and life for the dog becomes an interesting adventure, full of surprises, full of enjoyment, and an ever-lasting desire to try to grasp what you want him to do. The older dog watches you with bright alert eyes, to see what this silly person is going to ask next. Sometimes he laughs at you —a kindly, rather patronizing laugh. I've seen it so often, enjoyed it, and laughed back.

Once I sent my old bitch to find a snipe which I was convinced had dropped in a certain patch of thick rushes. She hunted diligently for some time, then came back with a clear conscience and smilingly told me it wasn't there. I said, 'Nonsense, you haven't looked properly,' and sent her back again. She shrugged her shoulders and went. The result was the same. So I told her I *knew* it must be somewhere near by, and asked her just to have another look. At first she was rather annoyed that I should doubt her word and her wonderful nose, but then she looked round with a very roguish smile, performed a sort of dance into the rushes, and with a grand flourish and a scream of laughter produced into my hand—a spent cartridge! This was, I think, an almost human subtlety, meaning, 'If you're going to be funny, well, I can be funny too. Let's all be funny.' And you know, she was right, as she always was. Later she found that snipe in quite a different patch, and I had to apologize most humbly, not for the first time either. In fairness to her abilities I ought to explain that she was an Alsatian.

Oh, yes, they laugh at you, and well they may sometimes. Mine are very good at it, though they don't have as many causes as they did. Your dog laughs at you too, doesn't he? But his is the laugh of triumph, of dictatorship, of the power he wields over the indulgent human who gives him everything he asks for, and demands nothing in return. He laughs when he runs away, or steals the food off the table, or tears up a valuable book. Yes, he has good reason to laugh. However, I hope you're going to change all that.

To return to the training. There are many variations which can be developed from the few things the dog knows already, and several further useful lessons connected with them. Going through a door or gate, for example. You didn't think, did you, that your dog should never rush through the door in front of you every time you are going out? Don't you think there's room for improvement here? It would be nicer if he followed you quietly, however much he wants to rush past. Right. A little practice then. Sit your dog two yards from a closed door. Give the sit command, and 'Back' if you use that expression as well. Then open the door very slowly. If he rushes or moves, shut it quickly in his face, and scold a the same time. Put him back in position and repeat, until he is quite still though the door is wide open. Go through yourself, and then call him, making him sit again when he arrives. Continue with this a few times, and when he's quite proof against rushing, bring him slowly at your heel towards the door, and let him follow, not precede you, through it. If you keep him strictly to this schedule for a short time, he'll do it on his own quite soon, and there'll be no more bad manners in this direction. The same applies to an outside gate, or climbing a bank, or going through a fence. Also, if you remember, the car-training taught the preliminaries to this lesson.

I should mention that the many lessons I've so far described needn't by any means be taught to the same dog. There's no need to imagine that you must teach your dog everything or all of them. I only suggest that you may consider at any rate some, in order to improve and civilize your dog. Teach him the few that particularly suit your and his circumstances, conditions, and life.

And here I must give a warning. Don't over-train. This is a most difficult thing to describe on paper, or even in words. It's more a condition of instinct and atmosphere than anything else, and the signs are detected only through long experience. You can completely spoil a promising puppy by over-training, perhaps spoil him for ever. Briefly, the danger occurs in two ways. (1) By teaching the puppy too many lessons at once, and (2) By repeating a lesson too long, or asking him to perform the same thing too often in succession. Both mistakes are usually made by novices, especially the latter. The first is mainly avoided by the inter-connected system I've described, but the second needs further analysis.

Generally speaking, purely disciplinary lessons may be repeated as often as necessary during one session, provided you leave off on a successful result. It doesn't matter much on these occasions if the puppy does become bored, because you wouldn't expect him to be exactly amused at having to stay in the same place, or go into his kennel when ordered. No, that's not the danger. The real danger is connected with the things you ask him to do which require his active and willing co-operation. If you lose that, you risk losing all the value of training.

The best example of this is retrieving, or some similar performance which demands the dog's own effort. And it may be through his very success that you ruin his immediate future. Suppose he does a simple elementary retrieve in a most perfect manner. You are delighted. Instead of repeating this perhaps once more—personally I shouldn't—you are so pleased and hopeful that you ask him to go on to do several other more difficult things before he has learnt the first properly. Or you are tempted to show off his performance several times to someone else. To your surprise, he suddenly refuses to go out at all, in spite of all persuasion. And perhaps next day he won't go either, and you wonder why. It was because you went on too long, in your inexperience. You weren't content to rest on success, but wanted brilliance and further success. Instead you had failure, and the risk of a ruined puppy. Well, never mind. It happens to me too. Give him a long rest and no work for a week or two. When you start, start from the beginning again, and hope for the best. The symptoms of over-training must be watched for. They are lack of interest, a sulky or cringing demeanour, an unwillingness, and sometimes sheer imbecility in a hitherto promising puppy.

Chapter 7

FREE WORK AND PRELIMINARY RETRIEVING

Discipline and Free Work

At first there are two sharply defined branches of training, and so far I have only talked about one, that of routine, more or less mechanical exercises entirely concerned with commands and the invariable response to those commands. In this side of training your dog uses the minimum of thought or individual reasoning. You don't want thought, you want obedience, prompt obedience in all circumstances. And you, as well as the dog, can be taught these set rules quite easily. Any novice who tries hard enough, has patience, and follows a system, can teach his dog to be under control. It's rather like going through a book of rules which require no particular instinct, gift, or genius to carry out.

You may have noticed that I have rather purposely avoided mention of this other branch of training till now. Because, though this should continue just as importantly through the dog's youth and adolescence, it must be treated at first as a quite separate thing. Later the two branches combine into what makes the perfect working performance.

The routine training is serious, there must be no joking during the actual carrying out of the various exercises. It's a thing of suppression, tending to quieten the puppy's natural spirits and independence. Now the other training is exactly the opposite. In this you want to encourage independent action and free co-operation. You must have the puppy's goodwill in order to achieve even the smallest trifle. Without that, you can do nothing. Instead of suppression you want expression, in place of stern discouragement, joyous encouragement. In the early stages it's important to keep discipline and free work separate, and try to clear the puppy's mind of all idea of tedious lessons when you want him to do anything demanding enterprise and action. In one case you order, in the other you request.

Before I go further, I'd better confess that the ideas I'm giving you are largely my own, and probably quite unorthodox and controversial. But they have worked very well in practice in the case of several breeds and many individuals. If they succeed with mine, they should with yours. No one can really find out from textbooks how to make his dog arrive at certain results. Practical experience is worth twenty books, so I can only give you my suggestions, all of which have been tried and found successful, and you must improve on them yourself. Perhaps many people wouldn't agree about these two branches of training. They might tell you that everything the dog learns is a disciplinary lesson. But then they seldom start as early as I do. It never seems to occur to anyone to train his puppy at eight weeks old. Yet my most successful dogs have been started at that age, and educated slowly until an efficient state is reached. Of course, there's a greater danger of spoiling the puppy or overtraining, but the symptoms can be watched for, and training immediately slackened or temporarily ceased altogether.

Dogs are endowed with gifts of learning and carrying out performances in greater or less degrees, just as people themselves are slow- or quick-witted. Naturally it's desirable to pick out a promising one in the beginning if possible. They'll all respond to routine and discipline sooner or later. But when you come to a test of their gifts in other directions, some learn almost at once and see what you want them to do, others are like half-witted village idiots. Happily for me I breed my own workers, so can reject unpromising material. I don't believe in wasting a lot of time over a stupid puppy when I can have a brilliant one. I don't believe, for instance, in spending weeks in trying to teach an unwilling dog to retrieve when I know there are so many who will do it naturally as soon as they can run about. You, on the other hand, may not be quite so lucky in your range of choice. You may have to buy, in the beginning, from outside; but remember, if you'd chosen a bitch instead of a dog, you'd have had a family of your own from which to choose the most promising material next time.

Seeking, finding, and retrieving form the basis of many later performances, whether your dog does them as useful tricks, or mine as work in the shooting-field. And it is in these things that you look for enterprise in the dog, so try to encourage the atmosphere of a game, making the game as amusing and interesting as possible. Very slowly the game grows into a habit, not a suppressed one, trained into the dog by a series of disciplinary lessons, but a habit self-acquired, which is a different matter.

It should be said at once that unless your puppy possesses at least some natural ability and hereditary instinct, you can't train him by this early method, but must postpone the retrieving until later on, when there are several other ways of gaining results. I should emphasize, though, that there's no reason why an ordinarily bright puppy shouldn't respond to this early treatment, and I think it's by far the easiest way to teach him.

81

Early Retrieving

Leaving the individual puppies of yours and mine for a moment, I'll tell you how I test every litter I breed. At six, seven, or eight weeks old I take each one out separately on the grass, preferably in a fresh place where the dogs don't usually go. I have a precious and valuable 'property', one that I wouldn't lose for anything. It's so old it might be described as an heirloom, and so successful and attractive it could be called a mascot. And it's just a very ancient fur glove. The interior is inhabited by a golf-ball, the glove is bent in half and strapped together. The scent from it must be strong, as every dog and puppy can smell it from a distance, and they all have a passion for it. As a preliminary retrieving dummy, it suits very well, being comparatively small and soft and altogether irresistible. I have this glove in my pocket when I take out my individual puppy. When we reach a quiet, undisturbed place, I take it out and, bending down, move it about in front of the puppy's nose. He may try to bite or play with it, or tear it away from me. I prevent him from actually gripping it, while moving it about, and then throw it a few yards into the grass when I know the puppy is looking. He always runs after it, and as he does so, I start to move away. If he is a natural retriever, he'll grip the glove and pick it up, vaguely wondering what to do. He sees me moving away and calling him at the same time, so follows, carrying his new toy, which he is unwilling to drop or leave behind.

I don't know if I'm luckier than other people, but all my puppies who have later proved excellent retrievers have invariably brought back this fascinating glove and delivered it to my outstretched hand, even at the age of six weeks. These are the puppies on whom I keep an eye. Others react differently. One will take no notice of the glove being thrown, and won't move a foot towards it. Another will rush after it, take a good sniff, and run off elsewhere. Or there'll be one who drops beside it and prepares to have a good chew. Improving on that, the next may take hold firmly, and make a bee-line for the kennel, so that his chewing may be uninterrupted. I hope to tell you shortly how to deal with these various reactions, but at the moment I'm only giving an example of how I choose my potential retriever. This is repeated several times a week before I finally make my choice. You, on the other hand, will have to make the best of what you have, only you see you miss part of the fun by not breeding your own family.

Always remember preliminary retrieving is a game. You may use a ball or a glove, but the effect should be the same. Personally I recommend the old fur glove because of the fascination it seems to exercise. It is naturally far more suitable for a puppy who has to pick up birds and rabbits later on. Very well, take out the glove, and see what yours does. Always show it to him first, persuade him to open his mouth several times as if to take it from you, or even tear at it. Keep it tantalizingly out of reach, and then throw it suddenly. He's certain to run after it. What happens next is an important and somewhat tremulous moment for you. If he brings it back, as you hope he will do, take your time in removing it from his mouth. Hold him gently by the throat with one hand, keep his head up, and gently extract the glove with the other. Avoid its catching on his teeth, or any tendency to snatch or jerk it from him. When you have the glove, praise him with all the lavishness you can muster. Such a result is pleasing beyond measure, but in my opinion, should occur with most puppies. After all, it's really rather natural. He wants the nice smelly glove, he likes the feel of it in his mouth. But he also wants to come back to you when you call him, so he brings his new treasure as well. On this first successful occasion you'll throw the glove again, after a short pause. First let him smell it, and when he brings it back the session will finish for that day, to be repeated on the following one.

I imagine this successful result would occur with eighty-five puppies out of a hundred. But suppose it doesn't? Let's see what the less promising ones of mine did. There was one that didn't follow at all, but just looked vaguely after the glove, as though it wasn't his business anyway. With him, you retrieve the glove yourself, and start the play all over again. Try to make him bite it, tear at it, taking any interest rather than none at all. Start a small tug-of-war which, after an effort on the puppy's part, he is allowed to win. You've then managed to get the glove into his mouth, and he is sure to keep it there for a second or two. Take it from him gently, opening his jaws with your fingers, and make him keen to have another bite, only instead of allowing this, bowl the glove along the ground. He'll be so pleased to see a chance of getting it himself that he's almost certain to run after it and pick it up. Then walk away a little and call him. I think he'll follow you, and you can repeat the gentle extraction. It's not advisable to continue or repeat this until next day.

With the puppy who runs after the glove but refuses to have anything to do with it, the procedure is somewhat similar, but you can throw the glove more freely than with the previous one. Quite a good idea is to play with it yourself, pushing it a foot or two away, and pouncing on it, until the puppy begins to see the thing must be more valuable than he at first thought. The chewing puppy can soon be persuaded to give it up, but if a little chewing will encourage him to pursue the glove, all the better for the moment. Wait until he dashes for the glove, then run as fast as you can in the other direction, preferably towards the kennel or house. He hates to leave his soft treasure behind, so generally follows at full speed, the glove firmly held in his mouth. When he reaches you, take it away gently as usual, and don't repeat the performance. The last puppy, he who makes a bee-line for the kennel, must be leisurely and unknowingly pursued, and deprived of the glove as soon as possible. As in the case of all of them but the perfect puppy, don't try it again till next day. This last case isn't really serious; and you can soon get him to come to you instead of elsewhere by a little lesson of calling him when he has nothing in his mouth, so that he'll eventually come after he has picked up the glove.

Progress and Pause

I'm imagining your puppy is very young, not more than eight or nine weeks old. Play this retrieving game every day, but don't attempt to go further for a week or two. Each time reach one or two successful results, and then finish. It's quite mistaken to go on throwing the glove because the puppy seems to enjoy it. Never be tempted into overdoing this game. Always leave off when the puppy is dying to go on. It'll make him keener next day. And all the time he is acquiring a habit, that of bringing to you what he has picked up, perhaps because you have used gentle persuasion, or because his instinct tells him, or even because he wants you to throw it again. It doesn't matter what the motive, the habit becomes fixed from a very early age, and will remain if you are always careful. Starting like this, I think you are bound to be successful. There are many ways of making older dogs retrieve, but none half so valuable as this early game with the glove, when the puppy acts entirely of his own free will, and really enjoys doing so.

85

Your perseverance must still exist, of course, as it does in the routine exercises. In a way I think this takes more out of you and less out of the puppy. You can't command firmly, as in the suppressing lessons; your concentration is all persuasive, your whole attitude one of asking, begging, beseeching. And never show exasperation or impatience. Just keep on trying, and get your results before the puppy becomes bored with you or the game.

As soon as preliminary retrieving starts, you can use the word which you intend to use always and permanently when you want your dog to bring back anything. 'Fetch' is as good as any, and you only employ it when you mean that there is definitely something to be found, as compared with 'Seek', introduced later, which means to search for something indefinite, which may or may not be there. In the beginning you say 'Fetch' as you throw the glove, and the puppy will soon understand.

After about a week or ten days of these first lessons, if you find they are successful, and the puppy retrieving the glove from farther away or thicker places, it's time to introduce a little change, at first so slight that it's hardly noticeable. Perhaps he hasn't yet learnt anything of the collar and lead, and certainly doesn't know how to sit still. As you hold the glove in one hand, ready to throw, you put the other round the puppy's neck or chest to hold him steady. Then throw the glove as usual, but keep him for a second before letting him loose. And it must be only a second, just the slightest pause before he goes bounding off to fetch the glove. After a day or two of this, you say 'Sit' as you hold him, and in an amazingly short time he will pause himself, so that you hardly have to hold him at all. Not only does he pause by a newly acquired habit, but he learns that 'Sit' means a moment's wait before being given the further command of 'Fetch'.

Thus your puppy very soon discriminates between two distinct words meaning totally different actions, one to stop, the other to go. By degrees the pause is made longer, but only when you can depend on the puppy's growing keenness to fetch the glove. This desire is something of a mystery. I can see no reason why a dog should ever want to fetch an object to his handler, yet his anxiety seems to increase as he learns more, especially when little variations are introduced by slow stages.

It is this almost imperceptible early pause that lays the foundation of the dog's later performances, because no dog should go out to retrieve before being asked to do so. Naturally this applies to gun-dogs more than any other workers, but it's an excellent thing for every dog to learn, even yours who is being educated for your interest and his development. I know many people let puppies 'run in' for some considerable time before they check them, probably because they think the puppy won't be so keen to retrieve unless he dashes straight after the object. This only applies, in my opinion, to backward or unwilling individuals, but not to the puppy who is normally keen.

There are several reasons why this early check is advisable, and beneficial, especially as it increases. You throw the glove while the puppy is watching. He sees it fall, and if allowed to go at once, he relies entirely on his eyes for finding it. But as the pause between the fall of the glove and the release of the puppy grows longer, he forgets, perhaps, the exact spot on which it fell, and only remembering the general direction, must use his nose to find it. This is excellent, but you must always make the pause suit the puppy you happen to be training. Don't, in the beginning, allow the pause to be so long that he forgets altogether where the glove has gone. The memory of a young puppy is equivalent to that of a very young child, and if you make the pause too long, you'll find that he doesn't go out at all, because he's forgotten all about it. However, you can judge this quite easily, because as long as his eyes are fixed intently on the place where the glove disappeared, he remembers. Let him go before this concentration passes.

Chapter 8

EARLY RETRIEVING HINTS

~~~~

Unseen Object. Other Objects

I know that some of these early lessons seem a little contradictory in places. But that's one of the difficulties in training; in parts it *is* contradictory. If your puppy, at any time during his education, seems to be muddled or dull, you must think out the reason and cease training for a time, because when there's any doubt in his mind, it generally means you've gone too fast somewhere. One lesson must sink in thoroughly before the next one starts. On the other hand you can give both types of lesson, the routine and the retrieving, consecutively on the same day; but always start with the free work first—the discipline comes later.

The next lesson in which you need the puppy's co-operation is searching for an object he hasn't seen, and perhaps doesn't know is there. It is, of course, a second stage of retrieving, and there's no particular rule about the time to introduce this. Your own judgment will tell you he is ready to progress a step further. If your training is based on the right lines, and so far successful, this development will come so imperceptibly that it merges into the other.

There are several methods by which you can introduce the searching for an object unseen. Earlier you may remember that I talked about a bit of meat concealed in the grass, the smell of which reaches the puppy's nose, making him instinctively look for it. This may be made more difficult by degrees, and you can use the command 'Seek' while he's sniffing about for the meat. Sooner or later he'll go out when he hears the word, knowing he must look for something, and as that something means food, he's only too willing to seek. But this method has several drawbacks, the chief being that it doesn't help the retrieving, in fact tends to hinder it, and it would be fatal for a gun-dog to imagine he could eat whatever he found!

After the puppy has become thoroughly acquainted with the glove in simple retrieving lessons, you might hide that instead of the meat, and it's more than likely he'll combine the two lessons of 'Seek' and 'Fetch', and bring it back. I think, however, that the seeking can best be achieved by a slow development of that pause already mentioned, and the gradual addition of one word to another. As soon as he thoroughly knows the meaning of 'Fetch'—accompanied always by a wave forward of the hand—and as he's doing his best to find the glove, call out 'Seek' repeatedly. Eventually he learns that 'Seek' means 'Look for something perhaps unknown, and certainly out of sight'. I have found this method most successful.

As your puppy becomes more proficient in the more complicated stages of this useful performance, you feel a warm pride in seeing him go out at full gallop when sent, casting himself about, testing the wind, until finally his pricked ears, waving tail, and alert approach show he's on the point of finding his quarry.

Now all this may sound very complicated, and not worth your trouble, but I assure you it is difficult to explain on paper, and that a practical demonstration would take half the time, as well as being far clearer. And it *is* worth trying these preliminaries, if only to see if your puppy takes to the work. Once you have accomplished the sit, seek, and fetch lessons, things become definitely more interesting. But these three things must be learnt thoroughly, so that you can depend on them, not only in your usual practice place, but everywhere.

Your next stage is to vary the familiar glove with other objects, until finally your dog won't refuse to pick up anything he can reasonably manage. I should start this variation with an empty matchbox, keeping it in your hand for a few minutes, and then throwing it in the same way as you did the glove. If the puppy is trained enough for the introduction of this, he'll usually bring it when he hears the now familiar command. But suppose he doesn't? Either you put it off until later on—an inadvisable alternative—or else you take steps about the matter. I recommend the latter, because it's as well to turn failure into success as often as possible. There's a rule and procedure I always follow on these occasions, whether the refused object is a snipe or a cigarette-case. The puppy dashes out on command, but when he reaches the unfamiliar thing, after one or two puzzled sniffs he comes back empty-mouthed to you, in spite of all your agonized entreaties.

Walk up to the object, calling the puppy, repeat the word 'Fetch' several times, hold him as you pick it up yourself, and then, opening his mouth as gently as possible, quietly put the object in his mouth. Be sure it goes in comfortably, and hold his mouth shut for a few seconds. As you keep your left hand under his chin, stroke his head with the right. This action tends to make him thrust his head forward, so that he tightens his jaws almost automatically on what is in his mouth. Take it away before he starts to struggle, give him a short pause, though still holding him, and do this all over again, never forgetting the word 'Fetch' as you open his mouth. Walk a step backwards, your left hand still under his jaw, and persuade him to come with you. If he follows willingly, continue the backward journey to the place where you originally started. Thus he has done involuntarily what he refused to do of his own accord, and the successful result has been achieved. The lesson is then over.

This is one of the occasions when persuasion isn't as effective as action, but the action must be taken with guarded precautions, so that the puppy is not frightened, made sulky, or discouraged from retrieving altogether. It always works and is, incidentally, one of the ways of starting with an older dog who firmly refuses to retrieve at all. It can be repeated until the puppy eventually picks up the object himself, and as he knows all about retrieving his glove, he'll apply the knowledge to anything. Here again, is a matter requiring judgment. If your puppy is not advanced enough, you must not start him on unfamiliar objects. I can't help you in this. You have to judge for yourself.

Seek Back

Once I walked along the sea-shore with a friend, taking my dogs out for exercise. We sat and smoked cigarettes in the long grass which fringed the shore, and after a bit walked farther until we came again to the road. Between this road and the place where we'd halted was a distance of about a quarter of a mile, if measured by the shore. When I reached the road I discovered my cigarette-case was not present, so concluded it must have slipped out of my pocket, probably where we'd had our rest. My friend suggested going back to search for it, but I answered that we might spare ourselves the trouble, and looked at my trained Alsatian bitch with a speculative eye. Then I bent down and told her something which sent her off at full gallop. She went quickly out of sight, but in what seemed a few minutes she was back with the case in her mouth, which she delivered into my hand.

Of course the bitch was highly trained, and knew quite well I had asked her to bring something I had dropped or lost. But this practical and superb demonstration of the 'Seek back'—so well known to obedience trainers—had one or two distinctive points. She had never before brought a cigarette-case nor anything resembling it, and the whole performance was the quickest bit of work I've seen from any dog. Not long ago this same bitch went back over many hundreds of yards of sandy beach, and found someone else's belongings which had accidentally been left behind.

Now, don't you think you'd like *your* dog to carry out this useful sort of performance? If you have followed some of the suggestions I've offered, I can assure you the result will be most pleasing. To my mind there is no 'parlour trick' more desirable in a dog than finding what you've lost and can't find yourself. In any case he's more fitted to find things than you are. He can smell them, even a sixpence in the grass, and you can't!

I'm tempted to give another example of this, which is invariably taught to all my dogs, irrespective of breed. Playing in a field with the dogs and puppies, I lost a very precious cigarette-lighter. It wasn't a cheap, ordinary lighter, but one of the expensive sort which so delights your heart when a generous relative sends it for Christmas. It was an impossible place, deep grass, and I'd been walking all over it. I put the puppies away, and told four dogs—two Alsatians and two Welsh Corgis—that I'd lost something special and wanted them to find it. They all dashed off in various directions, busily searching, while I kept out of the way and watched closely. Very soon I saw one of the Corgis pointing intently at something in the grass, just as she sometimes points a snipe in the rushes. I called to her, asking her to fetch it, as

I was almost certain it was the lighter. It was, and after a little excusable hesitation, she brought it. Now there was a case when I could never have found the thing myself. Since that episode I have taught them all about the lighter, and every one has had it in their mouth at some time or another in case I lose it again!

Every trainer loves to boast about his dogs and all the marvellous things they do. I suppose I'm no exception, but in this case I'm trying to prove something. You see, there *is* a practical purpose in training, and you'd enjoy working out your own variations to make them suit your particular life. But you will see also that unless a good deal of preliminary, almost dull, work has been put in first, no dog is fit or ready for demonstrations of his skill.

The 'Seek back' can be seen in somewhat circus form in the advanced obedience tests. Owing to limited and perhaps fouled ground, it's bound to become a little farcical. From what I've seen of the average seek back, it's rather a slow business; the dog is generally penalized if he deviates an inch from his handler's track, and also, I believe, if he uses his eyes instead of his nose. All of which is a pity. One really practical test, one useful accomplishment, is worth a dozen ring performances, but unfortunately the show obedience tests have to be fussy over small details—because competition is very keen.

You know, it's quite easy to teach your rapidly progressing puppy the rudiments of the seek back, which eventually lead to his finding your lost property. Assuming that he is now aware that 'Seek' means 'Go out more or less where I point, and find something', you can start when you like. You have the old glove—or anything else familiar to him— in your hand. Take him out for a walk, and wait till he's running ahead. When you're sure he's not looking, drop it surreptitiously as a thief casts away vital evidence, and continue for about ten yards as if nothing has happened. Stop; call the puppy; then turn round facing the way you've just come, and make him sit before waving him out to seek in the desired direction. He may go to one side or another, but he is more likely idly to follow your track until the scent of the glove comes to his nose. Persevere till he finds it. (I need hardly mention the obvious fact that you've walked *down-wind*, so that the scent is blowing towards you when you turn round.) It's really no more than he's done before in his previous lessons, but there comes a time when he realizes the subtle difference, and through experience and frequent practice discovers that when he's sent back, he always finds the article on your scent or path or track. By your attitude and manner he knows that this isn't the usual retrieve, but something special, and the quickest way to find the thing is to follow your 'heel' scent, wherever it may lead. Anyway, as you never start before he is proficient in the ordinary retrieves, it comes comparatively easily.

By degrees it's made more elaborate—longer, more turns in the track, and so on, including a change of articles. Until finally you have a dog like mine, to whom I have only to bend down, whisper, and she's off at full gallop, never failing to bring back whatever was dropped, though she may be five minutes or more out of sight.

Scent Discrimination

There are one or two things you can teach your dog to do later, as he grows more experienced, nearly all of them connected with retrieving. What fun, for instance, on a pebbly beach, to ask your friends to pick out one pebble from millions of others, and make a small pencil mark or scratch on it. You hold it in your hand for a few seconds, put your dog out of sight, and throw the pebble among its brethren at some distance. The dog is then shown the right direction, and of course brings back the right pebble. Simple, but effective. Naturally, from the dog's point of view, there's only one pebble on *that* beach, because he's looking for a scent, not a shape. And as far as he's concerned, your name, address, and possession are written in gigantic letters on that one pebble.

This is closely related to the scent discrimination of obedience tests, in which several people's handkerchiefs, gloves, and similar personal belongings are placed in a row. The dogs are sent in turn to find their particular owner's possession, which should be childishly easy for them in reality. If the dog has an average good nose and is properly trained in this, no scent exists for him but that of his owner or handler. I always think the failures in this test are merely the dogs who don't realize the handler wants *his* article, because actually the dog's nose is so sensitive that he can't make a mistake in this—to him—easy discrimination.

I wonder if you remember that paragon of all canine virtue, immortalized in the book called *Beautiful Joe*. Joe, among his many super-canine accomplishments, used to help his mistress put away the clean clothes which had come back from the laundry. It was his job to carry the various garments to the various people's rooms. And Joe himself tells us that there was no need for his mistress to instruct him as to what room to put which in. He knew, from the scent—(although the clothes had been to the laundry, mark you)—to whom they all belonged. When very young I was terribly impressed by this marvellous feat, in which I thoroughly believed, but I am even more impressed now, on looking back, to remember that Beautiful Joe with his wonderful nose was—of all breeds—*a Boston Terrier*!

In Germany and other countries where dogs are trained and used for police work, criminals are identified on these lines. A man commits some crime, and disappears from the scene. Perhaps, as well as leaving his scent on surrounding objects, he may drop some material clue. If he's obliging enough to leave his cap or other smaller article, the task of the police who suspect is comparatively easy. The suspects are lined up for the usual identification parade. But their accuser is no human being with a faulty or hazy memory for faces or appearance. Having been given his clue in the beginning, he is far more sure, certain, and almost infallible. If the man who committed the crime is present, and if in addition, the dog had a good chance previously to become acquainted with his scent, the dog can pick that man from twenty others as easily as you or I could distinguish a black man from a row of whites. In these matters a dog's nose can't lie, and every human being apparently possesses a quite distinctive scent. For this reason your dog should always be able to find your belongings, or follow your track, though it may be crossed by a score of others. The application of practical nose-work is nearly all a matter of intensive training and development of the dog's most valuable asset.

Now there's one important item I haven't emphasized sufficiently, but which applies to all preliminary retrieving, and should be noted well. It halves the difficulties both for yourself and the puppy. In order to be a successful trainer you must always study and notice the wind. It affects very closely all matters in which a dog's nose works, and sometimes the effects are almost puzzling. Actually we shall never be able to gauge the extent or range of the dog's scenting powers which, in my opinion, are wider than any of us imagine. I'll give you an example of this which impressed me very much at the time.

Someone was fishing from a boat on a Scottish loch, and when I'd finished my beat elsewhere I went up to see how they were getting on. Owing to various small hills and curves in the ground, the boat was out of sight as I walked to the loch. I had an Alsatian with me; the wind was blowing straight in our faces, and quite suddenly he stood still, sniffing deeply, ears pricked. He walked—almost ran—in front of me as though he were about to find a rabbit or grouse. And he went on in this manner, half-running, in a dead straight line, guided by his nose. As we came over the top of a rise, I saw he had approached in this direct line to the boat, which was on the opposite shore, altogether about half a mile from where he first noticed the scent of someone familiar to him. Similarly a dog can frequently tell you by his actions if someone is near by, though out of sight, or even a very long way off.

However, for the purpose in hand I shall only say one thing about the wind, which every novice can soon see for himself. In your first retrieving lessons make a point of taking such a position that the wind or breeze is blowing directly *from* the article thrown or hidden *to* the dog. He receives the scent long before he comes near what you want him to find, and it has the desirable effect of making him go out farther as he searches. When you see the alert, unmistakable signs that he is getting 'warm', leave him to it, and move backwards as far as possible in order to make the retrieve as long and distant as you can. And I assure you your puppy is just as thrilled and delighted as you are yourself, when he finds and brings back the object for which he was sent.

At all times study and think about the wind. It will repay you, and is of course vitally necessary to all gun-dog training, as well as tracking.

Chapter 9

COMMUNAL TRAINING AND SIGNALS

Communal Training

There's another way of training which is practicable for those who have several dogs, or kennels with puppies being reared, trained, and civilized. This is communal training, which is useful, not in place of, but in combination with the individual lessons. I have found it sometimes a great help with puppies who refuse to retrieve or take an interest in any moving object. Communal games, as well as discipline, prove a great delight to dogs and handler, because there's no limit to the variations on one or two main themes.

Puppies are quick to copy their mother or any older dog, and though I don't agree in general with working a young and older dog together later, there are many things puppies can learn almost from their first real walk in a field or lane. Heeling, for example, is quite easily taught in this communal manner. You take out a switch or leather lead, all the older dogs, and several puppies. The old dogs walk to heel, and generally the puppies with them. But as you go along you keep a wary eye on each side, and at the first sign of any puppy rushing forward, you swing the lead at him and shout 'Heel!' very firmly. After several days of this you'll find that even the youngest understand, just as they follow the other dogs forward when released. The lesson can be started as soon as the puppies go out with the others, before any individual training begins at all, and when the time comes to take out a puppy for a separate lesson, he can already follow to heel, which is a good point gained.

Swimming is another item which works better by the communal method than any other. Now it always surprises and amuses me when you tell me your dog or puppy hasn't learnt to swim. It's amazing that so many people tell me the same thing. Dogs don't have to *learn* to swim; nor do any animals. They just have to get used to the water. Not being choked by civilization and artificial habits like human beings, young animals swim by instinct. Their progression through the water is much the same as their running on land, and they don't even have to think what to do with their arms and legs. I always imagine that if a week- or fortnight-old baby were dropped gently into the water, it also would swim automatically and by instinct. Unfortunately, I've never had the chance of proving this, because for some mysterious reason no one will let me try.

Suppose you, your dogs, and puppies are on the edge of some water, preferably an easy step into a calm deep place. Perhaps you throw a ball out, and tell the older dogs to fetch it. They all rush into the water, followed by the puppies, who start swimming very well, but nearly always turn back again. Help them out as quickly as possible, so that they won't be at all frightened. Or you wade over some deepish water with all the dogs at heel, and once more the puppies follow the older dogs. Anyone that doesn't is left behind until he does. The best plan of all is to go out in a boat on a suitable piece of water, and call your dogs from one shore to the other. The puppies make a great fuss, a lot of noise, but they always come rather than be left behind.

All these methods are better than the more usual one of actually putting the puppy into the water. You don't want to teach them to swim, you want them to go into water without hesitation. They follow the other dogs naturally, and very soon think nothing of swimming quite a long way. When, later, you want the dog to retrieve from the water, he's so used to swimming that he goes out just as willingly as he would on land.

Communal work can be developed in several ways. I've already mentioned how I put all the dogs and puppies down and kept them back while I examined a sheep. This practical and useful lesson is easy enough to teach, even before the individual puppies have been taught to sit. Drop all the old dogs, and tell them to keep back. Walk away backwards rather slowly. Probably a puppy or two will attempt to follow. This you discourage by rather fearsome noises, and repetitions of 'Back!' Chase them back if necessary. After a short time they'll see the old dogs lying down quietly, and generally join them. This may be practised and elaborated until they understand. It's much easier than it sounds, and the results are always satisfactory.

My chief games are connected with balls, one or several. The dogs, however old and staid and gun-expert, adore these games, and never seem to tire. At times they get almost hysterical. The simplest form of game is a race, in which I throw the ball as far as possible, and they all run as fast as they can to get there first. Even though the fastest nearly always reaches it before the others, they try every time. Sometimes the ball is thrown over a fence, or into a thick place, or among trees, so that every one has to search diligently, and even the smallest have a chance of finding it. The most comical effect is produced by throwing it up to the top of a high oak tree, from which it falls in eccentric jumps, from branch to branch, finally giving a huge bounce

101

on the ground. On these occasions the dogs stand with up-raised faces and vacant stares, gazing into the tree and leaping round like mad things when they see the ball descending.

Sometimes I take out two or three balls, and when the fastest are reaching the first, I throw another in front of the smaller ones, so that they'll have a chance and some satisfaction. If there's a puppy or dog who normally and in cold blood refuses to retrieve, it's surprising what he'll do when by some accident of fate he finds the ball himself. He'll nearly always pick it up, if only to get it away from the others. And then, as he is so used to returning in any case, he'll probably bring the ball with him. Competition, if exploited carefully, is sometimes an excellent method of gaining results.

Ball Games

But the most valuable ball games are those in which the dogs aren't allowed to dash off the moment the ball is thrown. It's much more fun to combine this game with a useful practical lesson. Suppose the puppies will already keep back when their elders are put down, then quite a lot of entertainment is possible, and there's no limit to the variations. Briefly, the idea is one of hide-and-seek, growing more elaborate each time. I put all my dogs and puppies down, then walk out of sight. If a puppy is tempted to follow or come peeping round a corner, I shoo him back before I go farther, and make it quite clear that no one must move. I then hide or throw the ball somewhere out of sight, and come back to the dogs. They are all trembling with excitement, but I stand in front of them for a few seconds before giving the signal. On receipt of this there's a wild and frantic dash—real competitive spirit—and each dog rushes to where he thinks the ball must be. They search desperately, casting here and there in a frenzy to find the ball before anyone else. As a rule the oldest and most experienced bitch finds it first, but if she beats the others too often, I can keep her on a lead for a few turns to give the others a chance. Sometimes a puppy will stumble on the coveted ball by accident, and probably come running along when I call him.

Incidentally, every dog, young or old, is taught that once someone has found and is actually retrieving the ball, no one must interfere, nor jump at him, nor try to take it away. This is generally corrected by shouting the name of the offender. There's no limit to the places in which the ball can be hidden, and of course the game can be made exceedingly difficult; on several occasions it has been made so difficult that I had to buy another ball! Curiously enough, the dogs will obey both rules, by which I mean that on one occasion I can let them go after the ball straight away, and the next time make them sit first.

The primary use of this game is the encouragement and development of nose-work. But it has other valuable purposes as well. A dog who is retrieving something in a hurry is far less likely to bite or chew it than one who returns at his leisure. He wants to get it back to you before the others have a chance to take it, and so he generally comes as fast as he can. The finer points of delivering properly to hand and so on must form separate lessons, and come into later individual training. Another excellent advantage about these communal and competitive games is that the dogs never seem to become bored or tired with them. They'd go on all day if your energy —and theirs—lasted long enough. It's a marvellous way of exercising them when time is limited, or showery weather prevents the usual long walk.

I have a further development of the ball game, which is only suitable for the older and more educated dogs. Puppies

103

can be initiated into this whenever it's decided that their individual lessons have progressed far enough. I take out three or four dogs, and sit or drop them more or less in a row. Walking away some distance I throw the ball, preferably out of sight of the dogs, and then return to them as usual. They are all alert as possible, because each one thinks he's going. But I call out one name only, and leave out the hand-signal to go forward. If I'm lucky, and have practised this often enough, the picked dog will go out, the others remaining dropped. This may also be elaborated, and certainly requires much patience and practice to become perfect. The easiest way to start teaching it is to take out two only. Drive a peg or stick in the ground, and tie one of the dogs to it as closely as possible. Order both to sit, and throw the ball. Name the free dog, and add the word 'Fetch' if he hesitates. The other may try to go as well, but you can sternly tell him to sit. Repeat this experiment once or twice, and the next day you'll find that the one who stayed back will do so without having to be tied. Then reverse the process. All gun-dogs should be taught this lesson, not necessarily with a ball, but with their own dummy. Nothing looks more effective nor is more useful than to be able to shoot confidently with your two dogs loose behind you, and then send whichever you choose to retrieve the bird or rabbit, while the other remains immobile and steady. Actually any number of dogs can be taught this lesson.

There's one snag about communal work of which you must be careful. The stern displeasure which you have to show at times to puppies may react not too well on a sensitive older dog. The puppy needs a sharp vocal reminder, and seldom takes offence, but the older dogs sometimes feel ashamed when they hear the familiar terms of rebuke, and think it's meant for them, which is the last thing you must let them imagine.

Signals

So far I haven't said much about signals, and it's time they were considered. Now there are three effective ways of controlling a trained dog, all of which are sufficient and look impressive. They are really quite unrelated, though at times a combination is used.

In the first, a man will simply stand still, hands in pockets or behind his back, controlling his dog by voice alone. This is practicable in the obedience ring, where there's a limited space in which to work. It must be admitted that the really expert demonstration of this leaves an impression of thorough control and wonderful efficiency. The handler is like a statue, yet at his various words the dog does everything required, simply by knowing the sounds of the different commands, and discriminating between them.

The second and even more impressive is the sheep-trial man, who controls his dog by whistling. Every variation means a separate action, and the prolonged, almost ceaseless whistling at sheep-dog trials is music well worth hearing. I suppose of all the dogs working in this country, none are so marvellous as the trial collies, and few handlers possess such exquisite control as the men who work them. One man can handle two and even three dogs at once merely by whistling. Each dog has his own particular signal, and this method of control is spectacular to a degree. Even the small Highland crofter can demonstrate this in a surprising fashion, which is even more surprising when you realize that he takes very little trouble over his dog as a rule.

The third method of control is that of signs, to my mind a valuable one which is not developed and used as much as it might be. Obviously a vocal command is not practicable at any distance, the whistling is somewhat complicated and wouldn't be altogether suitable for a shooting dog, even suppose everyone were competent to whistle properly. But the hand signal can be made both silent and effective. It can also be brought to a very high state of efficiency. The more I train dogs, the more I rely on signals in preference to spoken or shouted commands. I have trained one special bitch to work by signals alone. So used is she to obeying these commands that she doesn't hear when I call, and sometimes I think she has lost the use of her ears altogether. In her case, this loss is of no importance. No matter how far away she's working, she looks up from time to time to see what I want next, and my slightest signal will produce instant action. I can even make her 'speak' by a sign practically unnoticeable to any human. She will now 'seek back' for something dropped without one word being spoken, because she knows so well the action that accompanied the words. I can bring her in to heel even though she may be a mile away. There's no need for me to whistle first, because of her habit of looking back at intervals, and when I catch her eye and make a signal, she'll come racing in at full gallop. I am training her daughter on similar lines with every success.

This hand-signalling is quite easy to teach if you start early. It's advisable to use words at first in addition to signals, but they can be gradually discarded later as the puppy learns the meaning of signs. When you tell him to sit, you raise your hand and arm. When you want him to go in any desired direction you point with your extended arm in that direction. Strangely enough dogs soon understand this indication, much sooner than is imagined. If you want him to go to one side, you start by walking to the right or left, at the same time signalling with your arm. Later you can sit or drop him at any distance when he happens to be looking or after you call or whistle to direct his attention. A wave of the arm forward will send him off again, and so on. Variation and surprise is always good for the puppy, so that he is looking out for your next move. All you have to do is to acquire a suitable visible signal to suit the words and action, and then gradually leave out the words. Thus you can control your dog at far greater distances than when he has to be within range of your voice.

Sometimes, especially in early gun-work, a shout is necessary, though if the puppy's previous education has been properly conducted, this should seldom be required. You don't start new lessons and trials of intelligence until the puppy is ready, and under sufficient control. In order to recall to heel from some way off, the signalling system is far preferable to continual calling or whistling. This can be done by bending down slightly and patting your knee when you call. Personally I have developed it into a slight movement of the hand and wrist which never fails. This resembles the signal you give to the following car that you are slowing down, and has the advantage of never being confused in the dog's mind with any other command. Practice makes perfect, and I think you'll be surprised at the quickness with which your puppy learns what is meant by your various signs.

Chapter 10

RELATIONSHIP WITH OTHER ANIMALS

~~~~

Other Animals. Poultry

Many curious friendships have been known to exist between dogs and other animals or birds. It is interesting to have several sorts on friendly, neighbourly, or even affectionate terms. The dog's adaptability in this case is partly natural, but mainly a thing to be developed by judicious care and training. There's unlimited scope for him to make friends with all sorts of live things which he would normally chase and kill, and it's more desirable to have him on the best terms possible with them than to have to tie him up continually because he might hunt the cats or kill the chickens. But you must have a suitable breed of dog to start with. Here I may possibly offend many people by saying that the kindliest-natured dogs are to be found among all the sheep-herding breeds, gun-dogs, and even hounds, but seldom among the terriers. These latter have been bred so long to fight and kill that it's far more difficult to make them friends with other or smaller animals. I know, because I've tried. There are, of course, wonderful exceptions, but I shouldn't like to trust the average terrier with tame rabbits, guinea-pigs, or even cats. In any case, considerable training is necessary.

Bitches generally make friends with other and smaller animals more easily than dogs, which may be due to some latent maternal instinct. Whether a puppy is going to boast a wide and varied friendship with odd pets or queer specimens largely depends on his owner's taste. Yet there are a few lessons every dog must learn, in town or country, so that he may be a civilized being instead of a rough and wild hooligan.

Your dog, for instance, might chase and kill hens or chickens at the slightest chance, not to mention hunting cats and dashing after sheep. You may think it funny and amusing to watch him, but when you receive a solicitor's letter, followed by a law case and payment of damages, you won't think it funny at all. Paying for valuable poultry or sheep is no joke. Apart from that, your dog is a nuisance to yourself and others. It is as well to do something about it.

It's much simpler for the person who lives in the country, and has access to fields and farmyards, to train a puppy about other live stock, than for the town-dweller. But then a town dog has fewer temptations or chances than his brother in the country. However, let's look at the country to start with. If you keep your own poultry, the training is quite simple, because the puppy is brought up to see them every day. Even so, there comes a time, generally about three months old, when he suddenly develops a mad desire to chase the fowls and pull out their feathers, or even worse. Prevention is better than a belated cure, but you must wait until the puppy starts sinning before the training can begin. As soon as you see him chasing, take a lead or whip, pursue him even as he pursues the hens, and lay it on with no half-measures. Give him plenty of chance to repeat the crime, when you are out of sight, but always watch for the beginning of this game. It is one of the occasions when I find a beating pays better than anything else, and will soon stop

109

the desire for chasing. You have already acquired a special disapproving tone for this sort of thing, and quite shortly you'll find you can stop him by your voice alone.

This is where the experienced trainer and the novice are different. The former knows well that his puppy will start chasing, and watches accordingly. The latter doesn't think of it until a hen or a chicken lies dead and perhaps half-devoured. And if this happens, you have several alternatives. Tie him up on a long chain or rope, feed the poultry round him, and give him a hard cut with the whip at any attempts to chase. Or take the corpse and tie it tightly under his neck for at least forty-eight hours, even in the kennel. Let him know he's in disgrace, and don't talk to him. Or else you can have him loose as before, let him think he's alone, and wait for the fun to begin again, when you appear quickly to give punishment on the spot. Personally I favour this latter arrangement. He is caught red-handed, but before he has time to do any damage or draw blood. There are other ways of curing poultry-killing in hardened cases, and as each must suit the individual in question, there's no need to mention them. Quite honestly, confirmed poultry-killing is difficult to cure, but if the dog or puppy had been brought up properly in the beginning, there'd be no need for a cure.

Egg-stealing is another horrible habit, usually developed in dogs who are allowed to run loose, and never looked after properly. This can be cured by keeping a close watch on the poultry houses. The egg-stealer is very sly, but you must be more so, and you'll catch him in the act of his thieving. Don't on these occasions spare the whip!

Sheep and Cats

And sheep. At some time or another your dog will meet them, and he must be trained to treat them properly, with a haughty disdain, no matter how temptingly they may run round or from him.

Again, the country dweller is the only person whose dog will meet sheep continually, and he has plenty of opportunity to train a growing puppy. You must remember that one or two small dogs can harm sheep just as much as any of their larger relations. Ewes at lambing time can be frightened by a Pekingese or a Pom, just as well as an Alsatian, into a premature birth of their lamb.

A farmer who has sheep nearly always dislikes any strange dogs going among them, and naturally looks at you with distrust and disgust when he sees you going through his field, your dog rushing wildly about, barking at the top of its voice. And no wonder. If you haven't your own sheep—and probably you haven't—then take your three or four months' puppy to a common or public place frequented by sheep. And if this isn't available, a farmer will give you permission to go among his wethers if you tell him you want to train your dog to be sheep-proof.

If your puppy is the very wild and headstrong sort, attach the training-rope, and leave it trailing: but if he's normally obedient and not too bouncy, let him loose. Don't keep him at heel while walking through the sheep. Let him pursue his usual merry way, and purposely dawdle about yourself, waiting to see if he takes any interest. He may stand and stare at them, or give a puppy bark at the sight of something new. He may even run away—and I hope he does! But probably he'll go after them at some time or another, perhaps in quite a playful way. Make your disapproving sound, and call him back. If that doesn't work, and he's on the rope, pull him in and give him a mild chastisement. If he's loose, wait till you have a good chance to catch him, and deliver the same. Then repeat the performance all over again. Fit the punishment to the crime, to the dog, and to the seriousness of his misdemeanour. In many cases a severe scolding will suffice.

The same rules apply to cattle. When you're training your dog or young retriever puppy in later stages, make him work among sheep or cattle, because he may have to do so when his work is serious. As a rule there isn't much trouble with cattle, because puppies are frightened of them. But there's nothing more disgusting to a trainer's mind than to see a dog rushing madly after livestock of any sort. It's a sign of a thoroughly inadequate education, and is no better than savagery. Hounds are always carefully taught to ignore every domestic animal, and their punishment for wrong-doing in this direction is the same as I recommend to you. Experienced hounds, in addition, are also taught to keep to their legitimate quarry. Staghounds may not chase foxes; foxhounds have to ignore hares, and beagles are whipped off rabbits.

You may want your dog to chase cats; you may even train him to do so (I thought this a form of sport in my young days); but as a general rule, I think it's better to leave them alone. Have you ever seen a cat torn to pieces by dogs? It may be amusing to see a good cat-hunt, but if your dog acquires a taste and habit for this sort of sport, some day you may be awfully sorry, just as I have been myself. My own dogs ignore cats, and as they haven't a household cat of their own, they have to be taught this, which is easy, as their gun-training automatically prevents them from chasing anything. The only time they are allowed to hunt and kill a cat is when they meet with poacher cats, gone wild, who live in rocks or coverts and poach game for a living.

An old house-cat, who perhaps has seen and known many dogs, will soon show a puppy his place when he becomes too bumptious or inquisitive. Failing this, you can teach the dog yourself by any of the methods I have described for the other animals. There's one other method, which may apply to cats, ferrets, or any other small animal. This is the formal introduction, and is generally practicable with older dogs. You just bring the two together, and introduce them. Let them sniff, and tell the dog this animal mustn't be touched. Have them together as often as possible, until a natural understanding is reached. And always remember your disapproving reproach when the dog looks like chasing that cat through the bushes, or the ferret which emerges from the rabbit-burrow.

Other Dogs

In his everyday life your dog will be meeting other dogs. His relations with these must be dignified, courteous, or quietly playful, but neither aggressive nor too friendly. If anything is worse than the dog who habitually picks a quarrel with another, it's the horribly decadent worldly-wise individual who seeks his doubtful pleasures in the streets of a town or village, picking up many acquaintances of a regrettable character. Perhaps you don't know that some dogs can be as degenerate in their habits as human beings? That isn't because they're just dogs; it's because their owners never take the trouble to see what they're doing or check their evil habits.

Now take lamp-posts, the source of frequent jokes of a music-hall type. Here is where I score with my bitch, since she had no special interest in these things. But there's no need for you to have to stop every few yards while your dog investigates the ever-attractive lamp-post or paling. If you do, then you've trained him badly, which is the same thing as saying you haven't trained him at all. There's no earthly need for these frequent inspections, and certainly the dog leaves his sign as a mere matter of form, not as a necessity.

Have you noticed the amusing fact that the smaller and more insignificant the breed of dog, the more fuss he makes, ploughing up the ground, and generally telling the world what a giant is here? Anyway, you can cure your dog of these things quite easily. Take him out on the lead in a place much frequented by other dogs. Let him relieve himself thoroughly once or twice, and then start the lesson. You have a choice of two alternatives. He pulls at the lead in an effort to smell and investigate. Either you check him at once with a very severe jerk on the lead, or else take a whip and give him a sharp slap, at the same time jerking the lead. Don't be content with doing this once, but keep on with the treatment, and eventually your dog will be as free as any bitch from undue and trying detours.

Similarly, you must always make your dog or puppy come to you when called, even though he may have found a quite charming playmate and friend. In obstinate cases this can be achieved by the training-rope, but as a rule patience and a formerly instilled sense of obedience will repay very well. In addition, the average house-dog can be trained to show very little interest in bitches if his preliminary sallies and attentions are severely checked. If you can train them to control their most pressing needs for relief by being clean in the kennel and house, they can learn control in other ways. It's up to you to encourage and foster this power of control, and it can be done.

The fighter is more of a problem. This fighting instinct is certainly more marked in some breeds than others, and it may oe noted that the fighter generally belongs to a breed or strain which has never had to work under orders, has never been trained, and has absolutely no hereditary sense of obedience. Think that out, and you'll find it correct.

I've seen a collection of twenty or more Alsatians—only obedience novices—sitting in a row on a lawn, not two feet of space between them. Their handlers were at a distance, yet these dogs took no notice of each other at all, though they were strangers to each other. I don't suppose the collies at sheep-dog trials ever think of fighting; they're too occupied with their job to come. The same applies to gun-dogs. Working dogs have plenty to think about. Their brains aren't empty or ready for mischievous ideas. I do believe this fighting instinct could be supplanted in many cases by something more useful. It's rather a matter of adapting one sort of energy, and making it work in a different channel.

There's little cure for the confirmed fighter, though he might have been cured in his extreme youth by vigilance and punishment. Even a thorough beating from another dog or his master will, when he is older, make him no better. So, if you can, do have a puppy from a working breed in the beginning, and not the descendant of a score of idlers who had nothing better to do than run round the streets or lanes looking for trouble as an outlet for uncontrolled and misdirected energy.

I shall not here run the risk of offending the partisans of many breeds by telling you what *are* the working breeds. But if you look at the American show results in the canine Press, you'll see most of them there. The Americans are far more sensible in the respect of classifying breeds than we are. Under the heading of Workers are the dogs who really do or should work. And then of course there are the gun-dogs—not alas, the purely show specimens—but those whose parents have performed in the field. So you've plenty from which to choose!

Chapter 11

JUMPING AND ADVANCED
WORK

_____

Jumping

You may have seen the spectacular jumping that comes into some obedience tests, or perhaps photos of equally wonderful achievements in that line. You may even try to teach your dog or puppy to jump if he is the right sort of breed and size, though I believe even Pekingese have to scale a small jump in mixed obedience tests. Jumping is one of the final things a growing dog should learn. I don't mean the small everyday objects he must go over in the course of his normal life, but definite organized jumping, or anything out of the ordinary.

I'm afraid I don't believe in spectacular jumping, nor should I ever dream of entering a dog, however excellent a performer, in any high jump competition. I understand this type of competition is being abandoned, and not before time. Even the structure over which Alsatians have to retrieve is far too high to be comfortable or necessary, and puts a great strain on the dogs. Because high jumping, with dogs, horses, and human beings themselves, calls for considerable effort. Even the very best canine athletes quite often end by refusing altogether.

In retrieving, so long as you are satisfied the dog can

116

retrieve over a reasonable obstacle, that's all you want. And in jumping, if the dog can clear a good height in comparison to his size, why waste effort by making him strain over absurd barricades? I know for a fact that one or two of the star Alsatian performers in the past eventually refused to jump at all. If you watch them, you'll see how much they hate this unnecessary and unfair imposition. They land as tenderly as a steeplechaser who has also been asked to do too much. And to what purpose, after all? It would be far more practical to halve the height and see an easy, comfortable, and perfect display of retrieving over a normal jump.

A puppy generally teaches himself to jump by very slow degrees, and as soon as you see he's growing fairly proficient, you can take a hand and encourage him, not to jump higher, but to jump better. When you first go out for walks with your small puppy, he generally squeezes himself through wire fences and wooden gates, and if you follow my advice, you'll let him find his own way so long as nothing impossible is encountered. If he belongs to a small breed, he'll go on squeezing through, but a dog of a larger sort becomes too big, and can't go where he went before. Take a five-barred gate, for instance. The puppy crawls through the bottom space, and this becomes too small as he grows, so he must try, with shrieks and groans, to go higher until he arrives, falling on his nose, through the larger gap above. Probably he'll end by jumping the whole thing without touching it. This must definitely never be encouraged until he does it himself, and if he shows any clumsiness at all, you must make him keep to his lower gap.

You see, there are some terrible dangers in jumping even some of the obstacles you encounter in an ordinary country walk. With a wire fence, the dog generally goes through one of the lower gaps, and until he can jump superbly, you mustn't let him do anything else. The reason is this. If the dog is at all clumsy, if he misses his footing, misjudges the height, or takes off badly, he may catch his leg between the top wires—or planks—and either break his leg or hang in agony until you can get him out, not an easy job with a large dog. Barbed wire is another terrible danger. Your old dog will jump a fence made of this devil's invention, with hardly a run. Your growing puppy may also be able to clear the height, but doesn't realize the risk he is running. The slightest misjudgment is fatal. As I write I have an eight months' bitch with a tear four inches long through skin and flesh, a deep and horrible wound between thigh and stomach. This was caused by one little piece of barbed wire not half an inch long. Though she could jump the fence quite easily, and had done so for some time, she was careless, and came over a fraction too low. I've seen the skin ripped from the back of a greyhound who was so intent on coursing his hare that he went slap through the barbed wire strands.

A young puppy has no idea of jumping, no spring. And this is a good thing, because his forelegs are growing rapidly, his bone is soft and can't stand any undue strain or jar. He'll learn by himself as soon as he's physically capable, so don't try to make him jump before his time, nor ever try to encourage him over any jumps he doesn't like. Any adult dog of a large athletic breed should be able to clear the ordinary five-barred gate, even though he touches it as he comes over. I think most Alsatians are born jumpers, and probably most retrievers, yet neither of these attempts anything serious until they are well over six months old.

If you want to develop this later on, make your dog sit at a distance on one side of an obstacle, keep at a distance yourself on the other, and call him over, trying to make him jump as quickly as possible. This can be practised with quite a small jump at first. I don't believe in the handler going over himself, pulling the dog on a lead; he'll do it better and learn quicker if he has a clear space, and you must give him that by keeping well back. It's easy to find a place where there's no alternative but to jump. If not, you can make one quite simply with a few boards. A low wire fence is excellent if you cover the wire with sacks. But always be on the lookout for possible or hidden dangers.

Words and Actions

By this time your puppy should be a well-behaved and decently mannered animal, one that you won't be ashamed to take out anywhere, either in hotels, restaurants, or private houses. He should be quiet and unobtrusive, controlling all those natural instincts which you previously considered uncontrollable. His energy is consumed in the work he does. By degrees he's learning your language, your moods, your orders. He knows that when you give a command you're always ready to see it carried out properly, so he obeys at once because he knows it's no use doing anything else.

You can make him fit into your life and be a really helpful companion instead of an ornament. Encourage him to fetch all sorts of things, and you'll find that he'll learn what the different words mean. It would be interesting to discover how many human words a dog is capable of assimilating. It's largely a question of age, experience, and training, but I believe dogs could be taught to understand intelligently a great many words, more than we imagine. I experimented once with an Alsatian bitch on these lines, but perhaps more from the point of view of seeing how quickly she could distinguish between three words and the articles they represented.

You, for instance, could have your slippers brought, your gloves, paper, or stick, and indeed anything you were in the

119

habit of using regularly, if you had taught your dog the word belonging to the particular article.

Further Education

I don't think there's much more I can tell you about training your dog, and making him civilized. I should like to repeat that it's far more difficult to explain on paper than to demonstrate in practice. And I dare say it sounds more complicated than it really is, but the few hints I have tried to give will, I hope, cover most of the incidents in ordinary everyday life. Anything else is just a variation on the main themes.

You can, for instance, put your dog down in one place, leaving him there for an almost unlimited period, a useful bit of training. An Alsatian owner once left his dog outside a cinema in one of the large towns, enjoyed the complete afternoon programme, and came out to find the dog still in the same place, waiting patiently for his master. You can train your dog to wait outside shops in the same way, as soon as you know he is capable at remaining in any place by himself. The procedure of this training is almost too simple to mention, but in case you don't know, I'll give you a hint. Put your dog down in the usual way, give the command 'Back', and wander slowly out of sight, preferably behind bushes or trees where you can still watch him. I am assuming of course that he has already been well practised in staying down and back. The moment you see a sign of impatience or intended movement, you must rush out and show yourself, repeating your commands in a firm voice. Do this just as he's going to move, not after. You'll find, when you go out of sight again, he'll stay much longer. Practise this at some convenient time every day, making the wait longer every time. Don't let him get up until you come right back, and stand by him for a few seconds. Try it in fresh places; make people walk past him; and finally take him to more populated quarters where there's plenty to attract or disturb him.

The idea of stopping him *before* he moves is that on subsequent occasions he'll hesitate to start, because you always seem to appear round the corner at the psychological moment. The whole training of this staying back is based on the fact that the dog never knows when you are going to appear, and so realizes that the safest thing, the thing that always pays, is absolute obedience to orders. Anything else means trouble and scolding. It is significant that in obedience trials there are very few imperfect demonstrations of this, and the dogs concerned have to stay down for fifteen minutes, while a stranger moves among them, and frequently whistles to them as well in an effort to make them get up. It shows, I think, that the training is fairly easy to achieve.

You may say you don't want to make your dog into an automaton—a machine. Well, that depends entirely on yourself. None of the training I've described will deprive him of one ounce of personality or character. If properly used, it should encourage it. Over-training and bad or mistaken judgment can certainly create, not only machine-like action, but perhaps a cowering appearance, or even outright refusal to do any more. In these things you must be your own judge, and no one can help you except your own common sense and experience. If you persevere, you'll soon know when you've done enough or too much.

Although I agree in general with communal training classes, which teach not only the dogs but their handlers, I can't agree with the people who enter the same dog continually in obedience tests and trials at shows. I've so often seen the most brilliant performers fail because they're just absolutely sick and bored with the whole thing. They have to go through the same old tests so many times, and to my mind the whole joy of training is surprise and variety. This, above all, is what you get from the schedule through which all properly trained gun-dogs must go, and which even by non-shooting people may be practised and enlarged on every day.

The gun-dog who faultlessly retrieves pheasant after pheasant will have had the same preliminary training as the house-dog whose biggest job is fetching his master's slippers. The principle is the same, and this principle is one on which all training should be based. Absolute control and absolute obedience, coupled with the exploited natural abilities of the particular dog in question.

I'm quite convinced that you'll find real pleasure in giving these lessons, and the dog will enjoy them as much as you do. Your friends will congratulate you on possessing a well-behaved dog, one whose brain is being worked and whose natural high spirits are being used and absorbed in useful accomplishments rather than in mischief.

If I had to think of a suitable motto for training dogs—or indeed any animal—I couldn't produce a sounder one than the advice to start as *soon* as possible, as *young* as possible, and suit the lessons to the youthful mentality of the puppy.

Chapter 12

FOODS AND FEEDING

~~~

It has been suggested to me that I touch on the more physical aspects of dogs, such subjects as feeding, bitches whelping, and general care. I admit I hesitate to do so. For one reason, there are already so many handbooks on the care of dogs, and for another, I don't always agree with the detailed advice they contain. Any endeavour to modernize and improve all live stock keeping is most praiseworthy, but, despite the theories of science, if you interfere too much with animals, or take them too far away from their natural state, revenge comes in the form of many resultant evils.

My motto in keeping dogs is: 'Let them be as natural as possible', by which I mean that they must and should lead lives which tally somehow and somewhere with the sorts of lives lived by their ancestors. In my opinion, modern dog-keeping tends, more than ever before, both by intensive inbreeding and artificial conditions, to reduce the dog to an inferior animal, one that is heir to many ills and weaknesses his forefathers never knew. And this is a pity. So, in my own small way, I try to keep my dogs in a natural condition, leading natural lives, and not interfering too much with Nature's design and system.

Feeding is a controversial subject, because it stands to reason that each individual must feed his dog or kennel of dogs according to what he finds best and can afford—and what is actually available. For instance, most people will tell you that good raw meat is the best staple canine food of all. The dog is admittedly carnivorous. Yet it seems extraordinary that the Highland crofter and keeper feed their dogs on a main diet of oatmeal and milk, with no meat at all: and those dogs are perfectly healthy, can do a hard day's work, and seldom if ever suffer from skin trouble. Incidentally, this oatmeal diet seems to produce larger bone in growing puppies than all the cod-liver oil or raw meat which they have never tasted. One old Scottish ghillie, who had bred dogs all his long life, was quite horrified at the spectacle of my puppies eating raw meat. So you see, straight away, we find a contradiction in this feeding question.

That's why no definite rules can be laid down, and why I hesitate to write on the subject. Kennel owners themselves argue and disagree over feeding questions. One finds success with one diet, one with another. I can, however, give general hints, and then tell you how I deal with my own dog-feeding, which, judging by results, is always quite successful and trouble-free.

Perhaps the first and most important rule in feeding is a correct balance of ingredients available. If you have only one or two dogs, and expense doesn't matter, you can do them really well, because their main diet will consist of good meat, fish, or other nourishing foods suitable for carnivorous animals, wisely mixed with a smaller proportion of the best cereal you can buy. And here we come at once to another controversial subject. Many people advise rusks made of brown (wholemeal) bread instead of the more old-fashioned dog-biscuit or houndmeal. This is a matter of personal preference, and personally I wouldn't change my present cereal—of which more later—for brown bread or anything else.

This matter of balance is easy enough to work out and carry into practice, after a few experiments. Remember, you have one sign above all to show you if your dog's diet is suiting him or not. That is the appearance of the waste matter, which you should always take the trouble to notice. This should at all times be hard and firm, and never soft.

With your one or two dogs, the proportion of meat to cereal will be high. When you have a kennel of several, and have to consider finances, this proportion is naturally lower. Generally speaking, economical feeding means more trouble in the preparation of food.

(ii)

Nowadays feeding dogs isn't much of a problem, there is a large choice, including all sorts of tinned foods and biscuit preparations. Economy generally means the taking of more time and trouble, but it is often worth it. Assuming you have two adult dogs of a small breed, feeding twice a day is ample. (Personally I give them only one meal, as I do with the larger sorts, and find they do very well on it.) A small feed in the morning, preferably dry—perhaps a piece of raw meat, or a brown rusk, or dry houndmeal. The evening meal must always be the chief one, and that should consist of a mixture of either brown bread, biscuits, or houndmeal soaked with gravy to a dry crumbly consistency, containing in it the cooked meat cut up or minced. If you feed your dog with raw meat in the morning, give it to him in one large chunk. People may tell you to cut it up, but this is quite unnecessary. He'll soon tear pieces off it, holding it down with his paws, just as his bushy-tailed ancestor did in the forest; and actually he swallows smaller pieces in this way than if you had cut it up for him. The meat in the evening meal must be well mixed up, because otherwise he'd pick out the meat and leave the rest, unless he was a particularly 'good doer'.

Some days you may have a beautiful bone to give him, but let it be a suitable sort. This will be a large thick one with lovely knobbles on the end, which he loves to chew at. The best time to give him this is after his big meal, perhaps when you put him away in his kennel for the night. A dog's stomach is an extraordinarily tough thing, and the gastric juices can actually digest bones, but I always like to give the bone after a meal, as I think it digests and is absorbed better with other food. People have curious ideas about bones, some sound, some silly. We must go back to nature to study the elements of this subject. Imagine a leopard or wolf settling down to a meal of dead antelope or deer. He pulls the skin with his teeth, until he can get at the flesh. Some of the inside of the deer is eaten, some dragged out and left. He may start gnawing the ends of the ribs; these are chewed with the strong back teeth, and flesh, skin, and bone will be chewed together. He can go a long way up the rib bones like this, but the proportion of bone consumed at a time is fairly small.

If you give your dog a rib bone from a bullock or sheep, it is generally without skin or flesh, and quite a different matter, so that when the dog chews and crunches, it cracks up into nasty splinters, which are not very safe to be swallowed. The experienced dog will often spurn these splinters, as though he had some instinct about it. But puppies and younger ones shouldn't have access at all to any kind of rib bones.

I often hear people say you mustn't give dogs the bones or carcasses of birds. In my own experience, this is an unnecessary precaution, and I've always given them these (mixed in with other food or eaten after a meal) with no evil results. At least to adult dogs of the larger breeds. You'll notice, more often than not, the dogs will break off and eat the knobbly ends of the thigh and drumstick, leaving the nasty splintery middle bit altogether, which shows an instinctive caution of their own.

For one or two dogs you have a wonderful choice of nitrogenous foods, which can be bought quite easily from your household butcher and fishmonger. The butcher can give you sheep's heads, liver, lights, scraps of all sorts, large bones, and tripe. This latter you can either boil for gravy and feed cut up in the evening meal, or else you can cut off a good slice without the cooking, and give for breakfast. People sometimes forget that tripe has already been cooked once, and is therefore quite suitable for a dog without the second cooking.

The fishmonger will supply a cod's head, which, boiled down, makes beautiful soup, or sometimes he has cheap fish of other sorts. The flesh from a large cod's head can, if you take the trouble, supply enough for more than one meal, and is extremely nutritious.

So you can work out your balanced rations, never giving food that is sloppy, but combining nourishment with the necessary bulk—a dog must eat a certain amount of 'roughage'—and not forgetting the bones, which keep the teeth in a sound, clean condition.

Always give enough food for the bowl to be polished clean; remember too little is better than too much, and the general appearance and condition of your dog will soon tell you if you are feeding correctly. The larger breeds should not, in the normal way, be fed more than once a day, and that in the evening. Needless to say these admonitions don't apply to younger stock or breeding bitches.

If by any chance you've been over-feeding your dog, or his food has been too rich, he may refuse one evening to eat his supper. Whether this is a sign of coming illness, or merely a literal state of being 'fed-up', don't ask him or persuade him to eat. Take the food away, and see how he feels the next day.

(iii)

You may be interested to hear how I feed my own dogs. I shan't give you any financial figures, because you wouldn't believe them if I did! But I think I can claim to have brought feeding my small kennel of seven or eight large and small dogs to a fine art—sufficiently balanced proportions at a very reasonable cost, making the most of the available material in the three different places where my dogs have to live. I should like to say that I've had no trace of skin trouble for many years, and that the dogs are always in good condition, and overflowing with spirits. Also, they all have to work for their living, and no unfit dog can do that.

My basic food is a special houndmeal made partly at my request by an excellent firm of biscuit-makers. This consists of wholemeal flour and a generous proportion of cod-liver oil. You can smell it in the biscuits, which are dark brown in colour, and machine-broken to the size of ordinary houndmeal. These biscuits contain no 'meat', to my mind a source of many troubles in dog-feeding.

Other cereals are oatmeal and rice, both of which are a little tiresome to prepare, but excellent for boiling in meat gravy, and mixing with chopped or minced meat. The porridge from both these should be as solid as possible, never sloppy, and can be fed cold as well as warm. There is no harm in adding various vegetables, outer cabbage leaves or any waste greenstuff. I don't think they are particularly necessary, but they provide a certain amount of roughage. Personally I never use potatoes, though I know some people do.

In two of the places where I go in the year, the meat supplied is the same. Twice a week I receive a goodly bundle from the butcher, all sorts of scraps, including sheep's heads, tripe, sometimes liver, occasionally lights, and large bones. All this makes magnificent gravy, and the solid pieces are put through a mincer. The changes can be rung for three consecutive days—rice or oatmeal, mixed with meat, and then the biscuits. Sometimes the minced meat is merely put with the dry houndmeal. None of this food is sloppy or sticky, but just the right consistency, and every bowl is licked clean. Bones are given separately at convenient times.

Many people would argue that this system of feeding is too soft, yet my dogs do well and are always healthy. Their teeth are beyond reproach, I would also mention that hounds—very hard-working animals—are frequently fed on a porridge made of meat boiled down, with rice or oatmeal, than which nothing could be softer. Yet they do a strenuous day's work on this diet.

There is a little to be said about mixing food. Years ago, when our dogs at home were fed on huge square biscuits, these were always soaked overnight in *cold* gravy or water. It was a sound principle, as I have subsequently proved myself. Sometimes I used to soak my houndmeal with hot gravy, almost boiling out of the pot. Every time I did this, the dogs suffered, either in their kennels that night, or out the next day, with diarrhoea. After much time and thought I discovered that this soaking with a hot liquid was the cause. Imagine for a moment you have a bowl of biscuits or houndmeal. Over this pour boiling water. Let it stay for quite a long time. Then take out one of the biscuits and break it. You'll find that, however much liquid you poured over them, the biscuits are soft and sticky outside, and leathery inside. This leathery middle never soaks, if the outside has encountered hot water. The dogs can digest dry biscuits which they may have greedily swallowed whole, in the same way that they digest bones, but somehow the leathery consistency of this biscuit doesn't agree with them at all. Naturally it only concerns food larger than the fine biscuit meal on which small puppies are fed, for this can be soaked with either hot or cold gravy. Since discovering this, I have always put my houndmeal to soak in cold gravy in the morning, so that it's ready by the evening. When you mix houndmeal or small biscuits, you put them first into a bowl, then pour in the liquid till you can see it reaching the level of the biscuit. When soaked this will be of the right consistency.

In Scotland my dogs have a slightly different variety on the menu. Sheep lights are cheaper than in England, people don't seem to use them so much; as well as lights, I use quite a bit of 'white' fish, cod's heads and trimmings, herrings and mackerel in their seasons, as all these are much cheaper than in the South, and all excellent for dogs and growing puppies.

A few words about these foods. Many people say there's no nourishment in lights, yet they make the most magnificent rich soup, and put through the mincer are very suitable to mix with biscuits or porridge. A pudding made of rice boiled in the soup from lights, mixed afterwards with the minced lights themselves, is good feeding. But if you use rice, you must take a lot of trouble to watch it, continually stirring until it's cooked.

Herrings are boiled just as they are, heads, tails, bones, insides, and all. They are then mashed and mixed with the cereal. The soup from them is also very nourishing and rich in many valuable properties.

In this feeding of mine I concentrate always on balance and proportion. For instance, if I give something rich, such as herrings, I counter this by mixing it with thick rice or oatmeal, so that the dogs' insides are always healthy and never sloppy. As we buy whole large codfish cheaply for the house, I secure the livers, which are good to mix in with other food.

So my dogs could never complain that their food is monotonous; they all seem to thrive on this varied diet, and their skins and coats are in a sleek condition. Though it takes me some time preparing the daily food, I am quite satisfied. Above all, when people tell me how much it costs to feed their large or small kennels, I think of my own modest feeding-bill, and smile to myself!

Chapter 13

THE BITCH. MATING AND WHELPING

—⚬—

When you first buy a bitch, puppy or adult, do select the best you can, both as regards pedigree and appearance. For the sake of any future litters you may breed from her it is important. Unfortunately, people don't always realize that a good bitch is just as necessary for breeding as a good sire. It's almost waste of time to imagine that a fashionable, expensive, or champion dog will correct the faults of a carelessly chosen bitch; and if you are going to breed a litter at all, it might as well be of the best quality. Pedigrees are often most impressive on the male side, but tail off very sadly on the other.

This advice only applies to the more serious side of breeding, and there are several other aspects. Breeding workers is a slightly different proposition, but whichever you do, put a good deal of thought to the choice of a suitable sire for your puppies. Consider not only him, but his parents. In this matter, if you are inexperienced and a novice, you'll find that the breeder from whom you bought your bitch will be only too pleased to advise. It is in his interest as well as yours that the bitch will produce puppies of a high quality.

But there are one or two warnings which must be given. I've tried to point out that one of the most desirable charac-

132

teristics of your dog should be a good brain and working ability. To my mind this comes before other considerations, and many of the show dogs of to-day are fast losing this vital and valuable canine asset. The result may be a physical appearance which conforms to the requirements of the show standard, but the price paid is too high if it means depriving the dog of his mental stamina. And this is happening, and has already happened in many cases, even with the breeds who once earned their biscuits by sound, honest work. I needn't tell you what they are. Go to a large show and look round for yourself.

Generally speaking, anything that resembles close or inbreeding, though it may produce physical perfection, is a sure way to a weak brain and loss of mental powers. This may even apply to breeding back to a certain strain too often. So again, generally speaking, the outcross of your bitch to a dog entirely unrelated should be favourable to brain power and mental abilities. I've certainly proved this to my own satisfaction, but then with my dogs, character, quickness, and a faculty for learning come before anything else. In many breeds, the exaggerated points which have been evolved in order to pander to fashion and the show-ring have even deprived the dog of the very physical qualities which he originally possessed, and which were vital to the work he has now unfortunately ceased to do.

If you have a bitch, even only as a pet and house-dog, you should breed from her at least once in her lifetime. I should never keep a bitch without letting her have puppies occasionally, and I consider it unfair and unnatural to do so. After all, it's not so much trouble, and there's a satisfaction in gazing on a litter you've bred yourself that is indescribable. In addition, it's the natural thing, and your bitch will derive enormous benefit from it, mentally and physically. There's no need for compulsory old maids and spinsters in the canine world, and there's no reason for you to deprive the bitch of the functions Nature intended for her. Similarly, a dog should be used occasionally at stud, as a natural outlet.

(ii)

You never know when your bitch will come in season for the first time. Any age between six months and a year is likely. Bitches of the larger breeds are seldom bred from this first time, though it is more usual with smaller ones. Personally, I should do it with either, as I've never yet found it has done harm, from the bitch's or puppies' point of view.

There are a great many fallacies connected with this breeding question, some quite amazing and very unscientific. I've been told, for instance, that the puppies of a first litter are of no value: that a bitch having a family of mongrels will have mongrels next time, and so on. If people only thought a little, and realized that there isn't so much difference between the human and animal world in many ways, they'd understand that some of the same rules apply. Actually, a bitch frequently produces good puppies in her first litter, though she may perhaps have a smaller number than subsequently. As for a previous family—the result of a misalliance—affecting the next—legitimate—puppies, the theory is too ludicrous to argue against!

You must keep an eye on your bitch when she is likely to come in season. If she's in the house, this is simple, but in any case you'll notice that she licks herself a good deal, and on examination a discharge may be seen coming from her. From the first signs to the end the time will be roughly three weeks. You can take her out fairly freely for exercise until the end of the first week. During the second, let her out just three times a day, and keep her in sight all the time. Remember at this stage she is quite likely to run away from you if she sees a dog, and she won't hear when you call. Remember also that a mating can take place in a very short time when everything is propitious. If such an accident does happen, don't throw your hands up in despair. All is not yet lost, provided you are on the spot and can get the bitch immediately after. Do what I did once with great success. Rush your bitch to the house, and douche her quickly with strongly mixed disinfectant. For this purpose I recommend 'Dettol'. I think you'll find that will prevent any disastrous results, provided it's done in time.

When the second week is over, you can exercise more freely again, but always keep a watchful eye. At the end of three weeks the danger is past and your bitch is trouble-free for another six months. Occasionally a bitch has a 'false heat' during which, if she is mated, she is proof against conception. Then there are individuals who sometimes enlarge as though they were in whelp, and who at the correct time after their season will even make a nest and secrete milk. These are exceptions.

If you have decided to mate your bitch and have already chosen a sire, then the whole secret of successful mating is to send or take her at the *right time*. Many novices make mistakes over this, especially when they own both dog and bitch. Remember, the inexperienced dog may become quite disheartened if introduced to a bitch who flirts with him up to a point, but snarls and bites when anything more serious is attempted. The right time is between nine and fourteen days after the bitch has come in season. In my experience I have always found the tenth day never fails. But I have seen people muzzling bitches in case they bite the dog, or trying to hold an unwilling one in position. This is wrong, and quite unnecessary when the correct time has come. In this, as in all canine matters, Nature's way is best. It's surprising how a totally inexperienced dog knows his business without any human aid or interference.

There are many fallacies over mating too, some very amusing, and none that will bear recounting. Even old breeders who should know better have some extraordinary theories and practices. One item is worth remark, however, a fact that is substantiated by modern scientific discovery. The number of puppies in a litter is dependent on the bitch, and the ratio of sex in the litter (dogs or bitches) is the sire's contribution. Yet this doesn't mean that because a bitch whelps ten puppies once, she will do so again. Neither is it certain that if your neighbour's bitch had six dogs and two bitches by a certain dog, yours will do the same. Science isn't as sure as all that. But speaking generally, those are two facts. Possibly if statistics could be kept on the sex-ratio of a certain stud-dog's progeny, it would be found to bear out the theory.

(iii)

The period of gestation for a bitch is sixty-three days, though there may be a deviation either way of a few days, and in some cases a week. Your bitch will lead a normal life for six weeks, after which she will become naturally quieter, more sedate, and her appetite improves as the unborn family makes more demands on her. You should know as a rule by her appearance if she is in whelp after five weeks.

During the last two or three weeks you feed her twice a day at least. Add milk to her diet as well, as much as she will drink. Even though she doesn't like it normally, she'll take it now and enjoy it. Cod-liver oil is another item I add to the daily menu, as I believe this to be of value to the development of the litter. There are a number of specially made preparations, generally containing some proportion of calcium, that are given to pregnant bitches. Give what you think fit, or what the vet advises, but not too many mixtures at once! If a move from one kennel to another is necessary, it should be done at least two weeks or ten days before the whelping is due. For a bed, give her a box, not too large, but roomy enough for her to turn round in. This should have low sides. I use for bedding, a layer of clean sacks, the top one secured by tacks or nails to the bottom of the box.

Towards the end of the time, keep a fairly close eye on her: don't force her to exercise, but let her do as she likes about it. One evening she may stay in the kennel when you call her out to feed. She probably won't touch the food you bring, but is sure to drink the milk. The time has arrived. In this, as in other matters, I still let Nature do her part without any interference. I can't agree with all the artificial and unnecessary fuss some breeders make over whelping, so long as it's obviously normal, and I shouldn't like to say how many litters I've bred. In the old days our bitches merely used to creep into the nest in the stables or hayloft, unseen by any human eye, and have their families in peace. This was how it should be. I do, however, concede a little to the modern fashion, because I like to stay and see the first puppy safely born. After this, having left a bowl of milk for the bitch, I leave her in peace till the morning, or for such time as she reasonably wants to complete her task. The majority of healthy bitches whelp easily and naturally, but of course there are occasions when things go wrong. Suppose your bitch strains for a long time—anything over two hours is dangerous—without result. Then don't hesitate to summon the vet as quickly as possible. In fact, in all times of serious doubt, rely on professional assistance if you value your animals.

If by any chance a bitch whelps too soon, even a week, not much harm is done. The last two litters I bred were born a week too soon. In these cases the bitch seems to suffer more than usual, and if the puppies are looking cold and lifeless, a warm box in front of the fire and a little massage will generally pull them round, so that they can soon be put back with the mother. You should make sure that every puppy is taking nourishment, and if necessary open the mouth on the teat, when the puppy will usually respond. Always remove dead puppies as soon as possible, without the mother seeing you do so.

Next morning, or whenever the family has ceased to arrive, persuade the bitch to go out for a short time, a thing she will probably object to doing. See that her bowels are acting, and they will most likely to be in a loose condition for some days. Give her all the milk she'll drink, and nourishing food of a soft nature. When you get her out for the first time, remove the puppies into another box for a few moments—on something soft—and take off the two top sacks of which the bed consists. This will ensure a clean, dry bed for her to go back on. Blankets or sacks are always better than hay or straw, but they must always be well secured so that there are no folds and wrinkles under which the puppies might crawl and be suffocated. For the first few weeks let the bitch have freedom to go in and out as she pleases.

Regarding the number of puppies and the use of a foster-mother, I would advise you, unless you have exceptional prospects of selling all your litter, to destroy superfluous puppies. A foster is an expensive item, and not to be considered unless it's really worth while. So if this is a first family, destroy the worst or weakest bitches, and keep the puppies you consider the best. In second and later whelpings, if the breed is one that normally produces a large number, most people will tell you to keep six. This rather depends on the bitch, but roughly speaking, the more she rears, the sooner she grows tired of them, and this gives you the trouble of weaning them earlier. I have one guide which

138

helps me to decide on the number to be kept. I count the number of (working) teats on the bitch, and keep one puppy less than this number. It's not infallible, but I give you the hint for what it's worth.

At three weeks old you'll start the family lapping milk. Do this when the mother has been absent for a spell, and thereafter give them milk every day, in a suitable quantity according to how they are being fed by the mother. You'll also have to provide a box or bench for the bitch to jump on when she wants to escape the too frequent attentions of her growing family. If possible, wean the puppies altogether at five to six weeks, though the mother should stay with them at night so that she may feed them if she wishes.

Chapter 14

REARING PUPPIES

(i)

Tails or dewclaws should be cut off as soon after birth as possible, the earlier the better. I always do this on the second day. It's quite a painless operation, and as the bitch is continually licking the puppies, there's surprisingly little blood. To cut the tail, sterilize a pair of scissors—there are some specially shaped for the job, but a good sharp pair of ordinary ones will do—by boiling in water. If possible, have an assistant to hold the puppy. With your left finger and thumb, draw the skin of the tail up towards the body from the place you intend to cut, and when you have it as far as it will go, make a quick, clean cut. Put the puppy back at once with the mother, though the operation must of course be performed away from her. Later, this extra skin comes down over the bone, and it all heals neatly in a day or so. Dewclaws are removed quite easily.

The same milk you have given the bitch before, during, and after whelping will be that on which you wean and rear the puppies. Here again, every breeder has his favourite brand, but if you can afford the slight extra cost, and only breed a litter occasionally, do try Ideal condensed milk (Nestlé's unsweetened). I think you'll find the puppies thriving on it, and it keeps sweet and fresh for a long time after mixing. Quite definitely cow's milk is most unsuitable for puppies, and unless mixed with a proportion of Plasmon, is no use. The reasons for this are plain if you look at the following percentages of ingredients:

	Casein	Butter	Sugar
Cow	4·5	3·5	5
Bitch	10·0	10·0	3·5

On this showing it seems strange that Ideal condensed milk should prove so outstanding as a successful food. The mixture I find best is one of half and half, i.e. one tin of milk to one of water. This is somewhat rich, but the excreta of the puppies weaned on it will show the suitability of the milk and the proportions. Goat's milk is also used for dogs and puppies, but again the percentage resembles cow's milk far more than that of the bitch.

As I've already mentioned, the puppies should be persuaded to lap as soon as they are three weeks old. This can be done when they are hungry. Take each one separately and gently push its mouth into the milk, when, after a choke or two, it will lap a few mouthfuls. The amount and frequency with which you feed the puppies will rather depend on how well or badly the mother looks after them, as bitches differ very much in this. When each puppy has had its share, put it down on the sawdust specially provided outside the sleeping-box, and wait until it has done all it should before replacing in the nest. In a short time you'll find these early-instilled habits take effect, and you are laying the foundations of house-trained dogs. The mouths will probably be covered with milk. I generally let the bitch in to clean up, but if not, use a squeezed-out sponge and do it myself.

If your kennels are soundly built, draught- and weather-proof, there's no reason why you shouldn't have equal success breeding a litter in the winter as well as the summer. Spring or early summer is the ideal time, because naturally

141

the more sun and air the growing litter enjoys, the better. But you needn't be discouraged by the winter. Puppies can stand any amount of healthy cold, far more than we shivering humans imagine. But they must have a kennel free from draughts or drips, and a nice dry bed, whether of straw, shavings, or whatever you use. Personally I think nothing can beat good wheat straw. As well as being comfortable for the dogs, it has a cleansing effect on the coat, and if changed often enough, keeps them free from all 'doggy' smells.

When your puppies are six weeks old, they'll be entirely dependent on you and your feeding. Now nearly all experts advise a long programme of frequent meals at this stage. Five or six meals a day at least. But when I follow this expert advice, I find my puppies firmly refuse to take more than four meals a day at the most, and I think this is sufficient for six-week-old puppies. It should be added that you must never leave food with them, but always take it away as soon as the meal is over.

You may start now giving stale brown bread with the milk, and puppy-biscuit meal, perhaps soaked with good gravy. Don't let them have too many delicacies at this early stage, because if you do you'll spoil their appetite for the duller things which are just as necessary for them. Milk puddings, or rice boiled in gravy, are excellent and very popular. Cod-liver oil is best mixed with the principal meal of the day.

At eight or nine weeks or even before, they'll have dry biscuit meal occasionally, and raw meat. Most people either mince or scrape raw beef for puppies. This is quite unnecessary. If you put a finger in one of the puppy's mouth, you'll soon see why, when you feel the needle-like teeth. For what do you suppose they grow those so early?

For your own amusement and the enjoyment of the puppies, buy a beef shin-bone on which some of the meat has

142

been left, and either put it out on the grass or else in a clean place in the kennel. They'll swarm over it like tropical ants, and not long after the bone will be quite clean, the puppies will be in a repleted, sleepy state, and the little teeth they grew for the purpose of scraping bones far more thoroughly than you can, will have fulfilled their mission. Give them this or something similar two or three times a week. You have tripe, hearts, or fish to mix with their biscuit meal at other times.

(ii)

Never let the puppies pull and bite at the bitch when she no longer wishes to feed them. This simply means you must make some arrangement whereby she can jump into the run as she likes, but they can't get out. This brings me to the question of a run. The ideal house for puppies is a large building, an empty garage or shed with plenty of light and air. The cement or brick floor should be thickly covered with shavings or sawdust, and in one corner a nice box laid on its side with a low board nailed in front, filled with straw. My own puppies, when weaned, go into a garage, the double doors of which are open all day, with wire netting in front to prevent the puppies from getting out. In this way they have all the advantage of sun, air, and exercise, while still remaining clean and dry. In the winter, on fine days, as they grow older, they are taken for little walks, or put in the dogs' field for a short time. This garage also serves in the summer, except that the doors are left open at night in hot weather, and I make a wire-netting run in the field as well. Growing puppies must have fresh air, and as much exercise as they want. The latter they will look after quite well themselves, provided they are given enough room. I feed them now with several dishes, so that the weaker ones won't be pushed out by the stronger.

People buying puppies have often said to me, 'And about what age will he get distemper or hard pad?' as though these were a necessity. But they are not necessary evils, and nowadays there is inoculation to minimize the chances. Most professional breeders make great use of the various vaccines and inoculations, but personally, I should never think of using them on my own puppies. They live in the country, away from other dogs, and if diseases come, well, they must take their chance, and let the fittest survive. In my opinion disease is one of Nature's methods of elimination, and I for one am prepared to let Nature decide, as she always did.

There are nowadays wonderful ways of giving animals artificial immunity, but this is to the ultimate weakening of natural stamina in live stock. This trouble started, as many others, through the evil necessity of financial gain. It stands to reason that if you can rear eight puppies safely instead of four survivors from some virus disease, you make more money. But in reality you are selling some animals that would normally have died in Nature's elimination test. The conclusion is obvious.

These artificial aids to cheat death aren't confined only to dogs, or even to the animal world, they are very general in modern times—the human passion for preservation, which seeks to keep alive individuals condemned by Nature. I don't think, in the broad view, that the effect on general progress will be a good one.

However, if you have one valuable puppy, and you live in a crowded neighbourhood, then have it immunized. A word of advice about inoculation. You have the option of taking the puppy to the vet for the actual process, and looking after it yourself when you bring it home. This means quite a lot of trouble, temperature taking, special food, and so on. The other alternative is better, especially if this is

144

your only puppy. Leave it in the capable hands of the vet himself for as long as is necessary.

About the virus diseases and other complications arising from them I have little to say. This is always a matter for your vet. These things can have a number of after-effects. On the other hand, careful and continual nursing, strict adherence to advice given by the vet or written instructions dealing with the subject, will often save a puppy's life. The chief thing to remember is that you must continue to treat the convalescent as a patient, and never think it's all over and cured until the puppy has been normal for some time. If you come to the stage when you have to feed a sick puppy or adult with concentrated nourishment in order to keep him alive, I recommend a mixture of warm milk, Bovril, and a dash of brandy. Bovril (or Brand's essence of beef) has immense sustaining powers, and I have kept animals alive with this, when they were at their lowest ebb, many, many times, and not only dogs either.

In all cases of doubt, consult your veterinary surgeon, unless the matter is one with which common sense can obviously deal. Remember also that though the dog's appetite is a sure sign of the state of his health, he can go comfortably without food for much longer than we can ourselves. Frequently it is his own cure for overfeeding or general 'biliousness'. But when your puppy or puppies refuse to eat with their normal relish, keep an eye on them, and if the fastidiousness continues for more than a day, take temperatures, and look for symptoms.

Worms are a cause of trouble. All puppies are infested by them, either pre-natally or later. I'm inclined to think they are born with them. You must free them from these parasites as soon as possible, which will normally be at six or seven weeks old. There are numerous reliable vermifuges on the market, and whichever you buy, be sure to follow the instructions carefully, watching always for the results of your doses. Generally one worming is sufficient for these young puppies, though later on you will be worming them at intervals all their lives, and I hope at rare intervals! I find the really healthy dog never suffers badly from worms, but as soon as he is in poor condition or run down, he shows all the symptoms of them.

A curious thing that always puzzles me is the presence of lice in the puppies you are weaning. Although your kennels, bedding, and boxes may be as clean as your own bedroom, these parasites make a regular appearance when the puppies are about six weeks old. This especially applies to the longer-haired breeds. Happily the remedy is a simple one. Dust the puppies thoroughly with any well-known insecticide, taking care it goes properly into the coat, and that will be the end of the lice!

When you sell or give a puppy to someone, be he novice or expert, write out a short summary of the type of meals he has been having, the times of feeding, and so on, so that the puppy will suffer as little as possible from the change of ownership. A pedigree litter should always be registered, and sometime ago the Kennel Club made it possible to register a whole litter for quite a small sum, so there's no excuse for not doing so. When any of the puppies are sold, the purchaser must be given the registration certificate, the pedigree, and a transfer form, in case he wants to show his dog later on. This latter must bear your signature in order to be valid. These forms and other information may be had from The Secretary, The Kennel Club, 84 Piccadilly, London, W.1.

Chapter 15

THE ORPHAN

~~~~~~

(i)

Sally, a very favourite Corgi bitch, died two days after whelping four puppies, in spite of every effort made to save her. One puppy had been dead at birth, two passed out the following day (owing I think to Sally's fearful pain and movements in the box). The next morning, when Sally herself lay unconscious, the remaining obstinate and tenacious child was still noisily trying to feed itself from its dying mother. In an hour Sally was dead, much to my grief, and she left me as a legacy this one orphan—an ugly, red-nosed, raw-looking remnant of life, just about three and a half inches long.

I had always made up my mind never to rear a small puppy by hand. A fearful business, a night and day affair. In addition to the minimum feeding-times of every two hours, there are the added difficulties of artificial warmth and—very important indeed—proper cleaning. You may successfully adopt an orphan of two or three weeks old, but a two days' child is a tall order!

I tried to find a local foster-mother; even a cat with newly born kittens would have suited splendidly. But as is usual at these times, no foster was forthcoming, and I wasn't prepared to spend a large sum on having one specially sent from one of the firms who specialize in these animals. I had already lost a well-bred valuable bitch, three even more valuable puppies, whose champion sire had cost a goodly sum. So if the orphan was to live, it must be reared by my own effort.

The first thing to do was to find a deepish box, about fifteen inches square. In the bottom of this went a rubber hot-water bottle. On top of that, and carefully tucked round it, one or two pieces of blanket, with a smaller piece loose on the top for the puppy to crawl under. (She took advantage of this at once.) I then bought the smallest sized baby's bottle, and a tin of much-advertised puppy-milk.

Now I've reared all sorts of young animals—the smallest being fortnight-old mice—and feeding with a bottle was nothing new to me. When the animal is very tiny, don't try to make it suck from the large teat supplied with the bottle, but make a hole in the top of the valve at the other end (this resembles a much smaller teat) and let it have its milk through that.

I put the orphan in her warm blankets, and left her for about two hours before feeding at all. Then I mixed a small quantity of the powdered milk and tried to persuade her to suck the end of the valve. She objected, screaming and protesting that this was all wrong. I persuaded no more, but left her for another while. At the next attempt she was so hungry she *had* to drink, and was very thankful to do so. Her tummy swelled visibly. The noise ceased.

Have you ever sat and watched a bitch with newly born puppies? To my mind it demonstrates a very remarkable organization and system. It has always fascinated me to the point of being able to sit and watch for long periods at a time. And this was lucky, because then I knew how to deal with my orphan as properly as possible. As far as I can make out, the very newly born family is sucking almost continuously. Whether with consistent success or not it's difficult to say, but at the early stage every teat seems to produce milk at the slightest pressure. However, for artificial purposes, every two hours seems a reasonable period. The instructions on the tin of milk told me that only half a teaspoonful would suffice for one meal. It's quite impossible to gauge that measure for one puppy sucking out of a bottle. Therefore I let the puppy suck until, when I pulled gently, the teat came fairly easily out of its mouth, its small tummy seemed firm and hard, and the hungry noise ceased.

The bitch with puppies licks them continually to produce the necessary functions. Her tongue has the effect of making these functions work. So I had a soft duster, which had been soaked in warm water and wrung dry, which took, with all success, the place of the bitch's tongue. At least it did for several days until I thought of an even better plan.

Fosse, my Alsatian bitch, although not filled with the over-developed maternal instinct of others I've known, is very sweet with young puppies of any age. She always shows great interest in everyone else's children, perhaps because she has had twenty-four of her own, and no doubt thinks she's an authority. Anyway, I decided to introduce her to the orphan when it was about four days old. Whether she thought that I had had this single puppy which smelt so strongly of my hands, or that it was one of hers that she'd forgotten about, I don't know. (I rather suspect the former!) But she adored it, did all the necessary licking as well as its mother would have done, thus saving me endless trouble, and the puppy from becoming unclean. In addition, she was quite worried when she wasn't in the same room as the precious box, and growled at anyone who came near when she and I were doing our nursely duties. The curious thing was that she hadn't had puppies for over a year, and was just due in season.

(ii)

The night arrangements for the orphan were a little complicated and tiresome at first. As I mentioned, the hot-water bottle lay on the bottom of the box, covered by pieces of blanket. I arranged this central-heating by a system of layers. All the blankets were used when the bottle was first put in. As it became colder, I removed one or two of the layers, so that the puppy was nearer the bottle, and never became actually cold. In this way the bottle kept warm all night without being refilled. On the bottle under the blankets was the bottle of milk, which also kept warm all night.

For the first week I fed the orphan conscientiously every two hours during the night as well as the day, and owing to my carefully arranged plans, I could do this without getting out of bed, as the box was close to my hand. All I had to do was to grope for the bottle which had been kept warm by the patent heating arrangements, and feed the child. After the feed, she was held out of the other side of the bed for Fosse to clean and look after, which task was as conscientiously carried out as the feeding. So between us we got through the first and most doubtful week.

There was no question of sleeping on peacefully in forgetfulness. In addition to the subconscious knowledge that made me wake, the orphan herself occasionally reminded me by a series of small squeaks. Fosse the Alsatian also knew, and once I put on the light to find her standing by the box telling me the child had been protesting!

Warmth and food were the only necessities of the orphan. She slept quite peacefully after each meal, never making a sound until the next feeding-time. If only human babies behaved like that, though I rather suspect if they were as essentially healthy as young animals, they might be quieter.

My child never seemed to be troubled with 'wind' or digestive disorders of any sort.

Now after five or six days I gave up the special and much advertised milk food, even though I was assured that it contained all the necessary and correct qualities and quantities for puppies. There were two principal reasons for this base desertion. The first was that it was extremely tiresome to mix in such small quantities, and if I mixed too much at once, it curdled at the slightest provocation. Several times the night ration, though mixed as late as possible, didn't keep till the morning. This was irritating, as it meant going down to a cold kitchen and making some more. The second reason was that it made the puppy constipated, a contingency not worth risking at that early stage. Finally, once or twice she refused it altogether. So I introduced my own favourite—Nestlé's Ideal (unsweetened) milk, which is quite simply mixed by adding water. Now it may not contain the right proportions of the various necessities, but the results were most satisfactory. This is the milk on which I wean all my puppies, and I have never found anything but good in it. The mixture I used for the orphan was one equal measure of water to one of milk, which is a good deal richer than is mixed for human consumption.

I admit I had misgivings over the sudden change, but they were quite unfounded. She took to her 'Ideal' with far more gusto than she had ever shown for the other, and at once improved almost visibly. Everything showed that the milk suited. In fact no one would have known she wasn't being fed by her mother. It is interesting that, in spite of many inquiries, I have never found anyone who reared or weaned puppies on this wonderful milk.

As is the way of puppies, the orphan grew rapidly during her first week, and never had a set-back of any sort. One thing especially impressed me. At the age of a week she had enough warmth in her own body—after she'd crawled under the blanket—to be independent of the artificial warmth. I had imagined that if the bottle became stone cold or wasn't put in, she'd have suffered. As soon as I found she could do without it, she did so in the daytime, though I used it at night, partly to keep the milk-bottle warm, and partly to fit in with my next plan.

At about eight days old she existed for four hours during the night without waking herself or me. In another day or so we managed to last from 11.30 p.m. till 5 a.m., and shortly after that, from 11.30 till 7.30. This was without any discomfort to the puppy. I gave her a rather larger feed than usual as a last ritual, and that, with the warmth of the bottle, managed to keep her asleep. This was of course an excellent step, and there was still no set-back, but a steady forward growth and improvement.

(iii)

At two weeks the orphan's eyes opened slowly, and soon after that she could see and hear in a very vague way. The previous curriculum continued until she was three weeks old. The two-hour feeds during the day, the hot-water bottle at night, and Fosse's scrupulous attention to the more unattractive side of this undertaking.

But at the age of three weeks various things were changed. The orphan would now walk in a drunken fashion away from where she'd been sleeping in order to perform a little duty or two. She no longer relied on Fosse's tongue as a reminder and help. This was indeed a step forward. So I moved her into a larger box, which was divided in half by a small piece of wood laid across the middle. On one side the blankets were spread, on the other, a thick layer of sawdust. At first I had to keep her on the sawdust after her meal, until she realized and appreciated her combined bedroom-

152

lavatory. Thereafter she never made a mistake and behaved like a house-trained adult dog. This at three weeks!

All this time she was as good as gold, a most model child without a grumble, and she still slept as her main occupation. At three weeks there was another innovation. Cod-liver oil was introduced into the milk, a small quantity in two feeds. I thought this might upset her hitherto perfect internal arrangements, but it made no difference at all, and I feel sure was a good thing, guarding against chances of rickets. After all, she would normally be absorbing quite a few extras in her mother's milk, because when a bitch is nursing puppies, she is given milk and food which are beneficial to the litter as well as herself.

At this stage the orphan became playful after a meal, and would lurch forward on wobbly legs, growling quite fiercely. She liked best to chew and bite a finger. This was rather natural, since she was starting to cut her teeth. It's unfortunate that the human baby can't follow the puppy's example. When your child is cutting a tooth—but need I remind you of the agony to all concerned? And when at last it's through, everyone has to feel and see the sacred thing, as though it were as valuable as an elephant-tusk! On the other hand, my orphan cut two whole rows at once: she took less than a week to do this, and never worried about it. Really rather clever, I think.

Now with a normal litter, you try to make the puppies lap a little milk from a saucer at about three weeks old. I didn't do this with the orphan, and for a very good reason. You might think it would have been easier to feed her in this way. On the contrary, holding a saucer for a hungry puppy is more difficult than a bottle. But the real reason is that clumsy lapping from a saucer tends to cover the puppy's mouth and face with milk. This is all very well if the mother is there to clean the face, but when she isn't, you can't do it so well yourself, and nothing is nastier than stale or dried milk. So I kept my orphan on the bottle until she was old enough to lap neatly, at about five weeks. From three weeks onwards day feeding took place every three hours. After this it's unnecessary to say more, since the orphan becomes like any other puppy, is weaned, and goes on to normal puppy food.

This business of rearing by hand taught me one or two things. First, that the single week-old puppy can exist and be quite happy in the heat it generates itself, without artificial warmth, provided it has something under which to crawl. Then I was pleasantly strengthened in my preference for 'Ideal' condensed milk as compared with a powdered 'special' milk. I was impressed by the quickness with which the orphan acquired good habits, such as remaining quietly all night without food, and using the special lavatory provided, never soiling her bed. I appreciated the quietness of a well-looked-after puppy, having heard various samples of the well-cared-for human baby!

One word of advice. If you have the sad misfortune to be left one or two orphans, and a foster-mother isn't obtainable either easily or cheaply, rear it, or them, yourself. If, on the other hand, you are left with a larger number, and they're valuable, I advise you to pay for a foster to be sent from one of the reliable firms who will supply them on receipt of your wire. To my mind, two puppies would obviously thrive better than one, when reared by hand. They would at least amuse each other later on, whereas I had to waste time taking out mine and playing with it, so that its strength and muscles should develop properly. More than two would be a bother, though of course it could be done if you wanted a whole-time job.

It's interesting to try this hand-rearing at least once. You can always learn something new, but I warn you, it will tie you to your house for some weeks, unless you have someone else who will carry out instructions to the letter. Yet there's a sort of indescribable satisfaction in watching your orphan grow, knowing that without your own thought, care, and constant attention it would have died, instead of being the fat, cheerful little puppy which bites at your fingers, rolls its eyes about, and growls with what it thinks is a fierce noise!

Chapter 16

AILMENTS IN BRIEF

I have no intention here of presuming to trespass on the preserves of veterinary literature by giving a long list of ailments with their respective remedies. This is quite unnecessary, because you can look it up as well as I can, and there are so many excellent books, indeed volumes, on the subject. Rather would I go swiftly through the better-known troubles, and tell you one or two practical conclusions to which I have come. Happily dogs, if they are sensibly kept, fed, and looked after, suffer comparatively little from illness. The one-dog owner is better off than the man who keeps a kennel. He can concentrate more on individual treatment and doesn't run the risk of continual infection.

Food and Drink

Perhaps my main rule in most of the slighter ailments is the one I try to follow in everything connected with dogs: give them a healthy, natural life, and leave all you can to Nature with a minimum amount of fuss. For example, if a dog has been having food either unsuitable or too rich, he may become what human beings call bilious. His own cure for this is simple. He probably refuses food, eats coarse grass, and after a short time vomits anything which has disturbed him. People say it's natural for a dog to eat grass, and that it's beneficial as an addition to diet. Maybe so, but I have never seen dogs do this unless they have something wrong with their digestion.

Although you must always be suspicious of a dog who refuses his food, you should never persuade him to eat, nor give him something better to tempt his appetite (unless he is definitely ill or convalescing). Leave it for a day and see how he treats his next feed. If he again refuses you should take it more seriously. I think, owing to the artificial lives many dogs lead, they are apt to be off colour just like human beings who live a sedentary or unhealthy life. But dogs can safely and comfortably go without food for much longer than their human masters. They should, of course, have plenty of water available.

And here is an interesting matter I have observed. During the cold weather and in the winter dogs drink surprisingly little, except when they are having hard work or violent exercise. They will even go for a day or two without any desire to drink. I have discovered this because I don't keep water in the kennels. My dogs are taken to a stream three times a day when they aren't out in their field, and several of them regularly refuse to drink for one or two days at a time.

In matters of diet and digestion with puppies and younger dogs you must be more watchful than with the older ones. There are several dangers which lurk in the background, and which can be tackled far more successfully if discovered early enough. I've no doubt that if a puppy is off colour in any way, he becomes automatically the prey for parasites, internal and external.

Parasites

If he has had distemper, or skin trouble, or any milder

form of ailment, parasites, although not being the primary cause, seem to fix on him, and soon gain an upper hand unless immediately checked. The under-nourished, badly kept, sickly dog develops these things as a result of his unhealthiness. Worms, fleas, lice, and even ticks seem to increase in this case, and naturally retard any curative measures for the trouble itself.

Worms

Dogs are seldom really free from worms. In the ordinary way they can be checked and evacuated by dosing the older dogs at least twice a year—unless there's any urgent reason for a more frequent dose. The puppies are wormed as soon as they are weaned, at six or eight weeks old. Occasionally there are times when this must be done earlier. You have to use your common sense about worming, but generally speaking, the less you dose dogs, the better they'll be. In a small way this is one of the many controversial subjects, as every kennel-owner has his pet mixture. It doesn't really matter which brand you give, so long as it is made by a reputable firm, or prescribed by the vet; but be sure which type of worms you are treating, round or tape. The latter is generally present continually in all dogs, but doesn't seem to do much harm to healthy adults. There's always the possibility of some of the worm powders or capsules being vomited a short time after dosing, but generally this is the excess, the main amount does its work. After an hour or so, when you take the puppy or dog out for a walk, he will expel the worms, sometimes dead, his bowels moving perhaps several times as a result of the action of the medicine, which in itself should do away with the need for old-fashioned castor oil or anything similar. You must always use your judgment about worming. I feel sure more dogs' insides have been weakened more by too frequent doses than by the worms themselves.

Other Parasites

Fleas and lice are comparatively simple to deal with, and in any case no well-cared-for dog suffers from these pests. They are simply non-existent in a kennel which is properly kept and scrupulously cleaned. The exception is that lice seem to develop in the cleanest of weaning litters for some mysterious reason. For fleas and these puppy-lice, you need only dust the dog well with any good insect powder, seeing it is distributed through the coat, and your troubles will be at an end. Don't forget to burn the bedding and disinfect the kennel.

Ticks are a different matter. I could write a chapter on them, so intimate is my acquaintance with these filthy insects. Especially they abound in Scotland, I suspect because of the sheep, whose insanitary wool contains so many parasites of different shapes and sorts. The whitewashed kennel walls in Scotland are, at a certain time in the spring, literally crawling with baby ticks whose mothers fell, gorged in the autumn, from the setters, to deposit their eggs in holes and niches. These small ticks swarm over any dog they can find, and attach themselves in hundreds on their unfortunate host. Disinfectant baths have no effect, nor sheep-dip, nor anything else but strong iodine. Because you can only attack the tick by poisoning deeply the place from where he gets his nourishment.

However, the usual dog-owner doesn't come across ticks in this quantity. If your dog has a small tick or two, either wait till they are large enough to pull away complete, or put one drop of tincture of iodine where the head enters the skin. Try not to give the mature tick an opportunity of dropping off in the kennel, or you may be appalled later by the minute signs of his prolific nature!

Strictly speaking, the two better-known forms of mange should come under the heading of parasites, but it will be more practical to deal with these in the next section.

Skin Trouble

There are many forms of skin trouble, some of which cannot be accurately diagnosed except by sending a scraping to be examined under the expert's microscope. Generally speaking, the tendency to eczema in its various forms is definitely a hereditary one, apart from contributory items such as diet, overheating of the blood, and so on. I've always been lucky in this matter, and I attribute my avoidance of skin trouble partly to suitable food, partly to my dogs' being seldom in contact with others, and partly to the fact that the strain of dogs themselves seems free from these tendencies.

Mange

I should say follicular mange is the least common of those ailments which attack the dog's skin, and certainly the most tiresome, since it frequently seems to be cured, only to break out in another place. This is caused by a parasite which burrows under the skin, deep down into the roots of the hair. The chief reason it is so difficult to get rid of is that few remedies ever eradicate all the mites or their eggs. Although my own experience with this mange has been slight, it has been enough to prove that a dog can pass it to his progeny in some mysterious manner, and also that in a large dog with a thick coat it's almost incurable. An old dog of mine suffered from follicular mange, and every one of the

160

puppies he sired in one litter developed the same symptoms as they grew older. Yet his kennel mates never had a sign of it, though they lived with him for a year when he had it. This dog was eventually destroyed as incurable, and I believe that's the best advice to anyone who owns a thick-coated dog suffering from follicular mange. You will probably confuse it with eczema, and your best course, when several remedies haven't improved matters, is to ask the vet for a correct diagnosis. In its early stages it never appears to be very serious, and you may not treat it with the respect it deserves for some time.

Sarcoptic mange, which is also caused by a parasite, is easier to diagnose, is extremely contagious, and is far more amenable to treatment. In this, the coat falls out, bare inflamed patches appear, and the skin is much irritated. Eventually the whole dog may be more or less nude. He should be strictly isolated, otherwise every dog that comes in contact will be quickly infected. For this the vet will prescribe baths, lotions or ointments, and be sure always to keep absolutely to all instructions, as some of the cures for mange are pretty drastic or even poisonous.

Eczema

There are several varieties of eczema which arise from several causes. As I said before, the tendency to eczema is hereditary, as can be proved by certain strains suffering more than others. It would be unwise to breed from a dog or bitch who was inclined to 'break out' at frequent intervals, and some dogs are never free from eczema of some sort. Experts say eczema is non-contagious, yet it seems strange that when one dog suffers from a certain type, the others seem to develop it at the same time or soon after. I refer to what is known as 'wet eczema', a very tiresome complaint, particularly to people who keep dogs for show. Quite suddenly a large patch of hair will remove itself, and display a moist corresponding patch of skin, which takes some time to dry, and even more time to grow the hair again. More trying still, as soon as that patch is cured, another may appear. I'm convinced this is hereditary, and that the progeny of a dog who suffered from this would also develop it. Painting with tincture of iodine in the earlier stages is most effective, and that must be followed by application of a greasy mixture to encourage the hair-growth later.

The dog whose interior is in a fit and healthy condition is less apt to have eczema than his pampered brother who feeds unwisely, lives in the stuffy atmosphere of a house, and doesn't get enough fresh air and exercise. Dogs are quite as liable to overheated blood as human beings. A weekly dose of mild Epsom salts mixed with the evening meal is a very good thing, and is advisable as an additional treatment for eczema.

There are remedies for most skin troubles, and as these vary and new ones are invented all the time, the best recommendation I can give is consultation with your vet when anything of this kind looks like getting out of hand. Don't, however, keep running to the vet for trivial reasons. He is a busy man, and has plenty of serious patients to fill his time.

Cuts and Wounds

In this subject you have the greatest examples of the advisability of leaving matters to Nature. I've had cases frequently when human interference only made matters worse, whereas if the situation had been left to a natural cure, all would have been well. There are of course some obvious exceptions, but as a general rule, in canine injuries or wounds, you should take a back seat and see what Nature can do before you introduce your artificial human remedies. Remember that once you take a hand with your disinfectants, bandages, and bathing, you are introducing something that Nature never designed, and the dog himself won't help you nor approve of the medical mess with which you treat him. Even the wound itself will change its condition, and not always for the better.

In my young days, when I owned many sorts of animals, I took this natural healing for granted, unless the injury was situated in some place the animal couldn't reach. One of my favourite bitches, savaged by another until she lay on her side practically unconscious, more or less healed herself in a week. A cat, punctured with shot from a vicious keeper's gun, isolated himself and still lived. Another, attacked by a pack of terriers and bitten again and again, recovered in a few days. I read lately of a horse's leg, badly gashed by a stake, completely healing without human aid. There are many examples, even among the wild animals who suffer from traps, and any open wound can be cured far more effectively in a natural way than by all your bandages and disinfectants.

The best example of self-cure I ever witnessed was last summer, in the young bitch I mentioned before as having torn herself on barbed wire. The wound was a horrible one to see, and was placed very awkwardly. The loose skin where the hind leg meets the stomach was torn in a straight gash, and when the bitch lay in a certain position you could see the inner membrane which covers the intestines to a deep and alarming extent. The skin here is thinner than anywhere else, and a similar wound in a human being would have had a number of stitches. It was over four inches long.

The morning after this was done I took the bitch to the

vet by car. I asked him to be quite candid about the necessity for stitching, and ventured the opinion that owing to the awkward situation of the wound and the depth of revealed inner membrane, it might be better not to stitch at all. After examination he agreed without hesitation, and in fact said he wouldn't care to risk it. So she went home without treatment of any sort. All I bought was a small amount of iodoform to drop into the wound should it become septic.

As this horrible tear started to dry a little, a longish piece of skin hung down the thigh, but I resisted the temptation to cut it off. The bitch, gay and bouncing as usual, was only allowed the minimum of exercise, and started curing herself. In a few days she had bitten off the loose skin, and by continual licking kept the wound open and pliable. She was very keen to snap at and kill every fly she saw, a thing she never bothered about before. In two weeks the wound had shrunk to one of two inches long, and after a month had passed a small scar was left. Now I can hardly find a trace of the scar itself.

I've told you all this in detail because it was an interesting example of what an animal can do. If the wound had been drawn together by stitches, the odds were that the interior would have become septic, on account of the position. This rule of leaving dogs to cure themselves applies mainly to open wounds, and those which are accessible to the dog's tongue.

One of the most dangerous results of a fight is the punctured wound, where teeth have penetrated through skin and flesh. Quite often this is placed in an awkward position, and in any case the skin nearly always heals too quickly before complete healing has taken place inside. This always means trouble. After a fight you must examine your dog carefully. Bathe the inaccessible tears and gashes with mild disinfectant. But the punctured wound must be kept open at any cost until there is no more discharge. This can be done by continual bathing and squeezing out.

As a general rule I don't believe in too much disinfectant treatment for animals' wounds, unless they are definitely of a septic nature. Even the mildest disinfectant is a slight irritant and retards natural healing. In our civilized state we are apt too much to rely on artificial treatment, forgetting that the physical body and the blood-stream itself have tremendous powers of mending if left alone.

But if a dog suffers from any serious septic wound or suspicious swelling, it's advisable to consult the vet, who will use his lance at the right moment. An old bitch of mine who had been attacked by another developed, from a neglected puncture wound, a whole septic back. This I lanced myself when I discovered it, and the amount of pus which came out was unbelievable.

Thorns or injuries to the feet are generally looked after by the dogs themselves, but if a swelling occurs, use a poultice and bandage. I find bran or bread makes the best poultice. When the swelling bursts, let the dog attend to it. A cut pad may be quite tiresome and take a long time to heal. I consider boracic ointment (with a bandage) effective in healing this quickly. Vaseline also is a help to sore pads.

Internal Injuries

In all cases of internal injuries, such as may be caused by a dog being run over, always employ the nearest vet, for these can be dealt with neither by the dog nor his owner. Any internal injury should be regarded with much gravity. Splinters of bones and other indigestible objects can cause much suffering and even death. If you suspect your puppy of swallowing anything of this nature, you should try to make him costive, so that the object may be expelled with the least chance of piercing the intestine. This can be done by giving rice or maize meal mixed to a thick consistency, but should the undesirable thing not be expelled it may cause endless trouble and probably death; though I was told of a spaniel puppy who swallowed a large darning-needle which eventually came through! Don't forget, however, that the appearance of blood from the intestines may be caused by worms as well as by internal inflammation, and try to discover the cause, because naturally the treatment must differ. You can't go far wrong if you consult your vet when in doubt, and you at least have the satisfaction of knowing you are doing the best you can for your dog. But common sense, experience, and lack of panic or fuss should prevent a large annual bill from this quarter.

Distemper

I have already advised expert advice on the subject of serious diseases like hard pad and its relations; this also applies to various ailments contracted by pregnant or whelped bitches. Precautions, cures, and injections for these are changing all the time, so no cut-and-dried information can be of lasting value. But I'd like to repeat that convalescence from any disease should be a long process, because so many types of relapse can occur.

As to nourishment, give the dog what he will take, anything he fancies, and be thankful he fancies anything at all. Small, condensed, and sustaining feeds are best. Here tinned milk is admirable, as well as Bovril, Oxo, or Brand's essence. At a certain stage he may not eat for days on end, but a warm drink mixed with Bovril, and a spoonful of good meat jelly will keep him going quite well. It is preferable to let him drink of his own accord, though at the worst stage you may have to help with a spoon; and at this stage I have used a small quantity of that immortal remedy for all ills—whisky —with good effect.

When he is recovering, never be in a hurry to move him or take him out too soon, even though he seems to be making marvellous progress. Just keep on cleaning up, and be thankful he is still there. A relapse is most dangerous, and will probably undo in a short time all your care and achievement. There are many degrees of these illnesses, and some dogs have them so slightly that you may easily mistake them for a chill. Continue with nourishing food throughout convalescence, and start exercise again by slow stages and with the utmost watchfulness.

Chapter 17

SHOWS AND SHOWING

━━━

(i)

Being very fond of one Alsatian lady (she who showed a sense of humour in another chapter) I decided we should together betake ourselves to a small show, just to see. We knew, of course, what the result would be before we went, but as our ideas of shows entirely tallied, we didn't mind a bit. In due course we arrived in the ring, along with a few rather inferior specimens of the breed. As we stood side by side, away from the others, concentrated entirely on catching the eye of the unresponsive judge, I heard a woman say to her friend just behind me—'Isn't she standing well? You can see *she* knows all about showing.' Secretly we bridled, but I always remember that comment as a compliment to the preliminary work the old lady and I had practised on the home lawn, because really we knew nothing at all about shows. I need hardly add that in spite of our joint efforts and perfect ring-manners, we only got a reserve!

Now I haven't told you this little story to impress you that we were anything but the merest novices. Rather I'm trying to show that preliminary practice at home will make you look experienced in the ring. And if you have an animal which may make history in the breed, you should concentrate on shows and showing. Let's get it right from the beginning.

You buy a puppy, originally perhaps merely as a pet. Your friends come to admire it. The more experienced among them will tell you the puppy should be shown. He's good, definitely good. So you listen to the advice and decide to do something about it. First you look for the various papers you received with the puppy. They should consist of the pedigree, and either a registration or transfer form. The former if the puppy has never been registered, the latter if he has, and you want to show him in your own name. In any case you fill in one or the other, and send it to the Kennel Club with the required sum. If you have doubts or difficulties of any sort, they'll soon put you right and give you instructions.

Go to shows; and watch the ring where your breed is being judged. Particularly observe the handlers of the winning dogs and anyone else who you think looks experienced. See what they do to make their dogs look smart, stand, and move correctly, and save this up in your memory when you go home. The next step is to buy one of the weekly dog-papers, and look among the lists of coming shows. Choose one which is not too far away, one which caters for your breed (preferably having more than one class) and which is quite a small affair. This is the best beginning if you are a novice. The secretary will send you a schedule and entry form on request, and you should read the Kennel Club regulations which are to be found as a preface to every schedule. Having done this, you enter your puppy in the correct class or classes.

Meanwhile you've been practising on your lawn or in your biggest room with your puppy. Imagine this is the ring, and if possible get someone to act the part of the judge. Lead the puppy round, seeing he is always in sight of the 'judge'. When he stands, put him in the correct position, and whether a rubber ball or a piece of liver makes him interested, use it to the best advantage. In fact, do as you saw the experts do with their dogs. In a day or two you'll get the puppy to grasp what you want, and he should pose himself naturally, alert and expectantly waiting for his reward or plaything.

On the day of the show, you must try to see he relieves himself before starting, and if possible again before you enter the show. Curiously enough, many dogs prefer to withstand and postpone their physical needs rather than perform in a strange place. You bring with you his brushes, etc.: and I strongly advise you to bring some of his own biscuits or meat as well. Personally I find my dogs never touch the allowance they get at shows, and I wait till they come home before feeding them.

You will, of course, have to pass the vet before being allowed to take your dog in. This is sometimes a swift cursory examination, but I warn you it's no use to explain feverishly that the patch of mange was the result of a fight! It just doesn't work, and if there's anything doubtful about your puppy's health and condition, don't take him. I might mention here the fact that in sending your entry form, you give your word that the dog or puppy entered has neither been afflicted by nor in contact with any contagious disease for some weeks before the show. Furthermore, you give your word that if he does contract or is in contact with disease, you will keep him away. I'm afraid this solemn pledge isn't always kept, and obviously it's purely a matter for individual honour. Well, never mind the temptation, don't make excuses to yourself, but stick to your word, no matter how much it disappoints you.

You have now arrived at the bench, and securely chained your puppy. Try to find out when your class will be judged, and where. Take the puppy for exercise if he has to stay on his bench for a long time. You may also practise a little in the show environment, so that the puppy will feel comfortable in spite of his unfamiliar surroundings.

There is only one person in the ring. That is the judge. Don't be over anxious or fussy, because that will be communicated to your dog and he won't be at his best. Just behave as though you were at home, except that you must divide your attention between your puppy and the judge. One warning must be given. Use discrimination in making the puppy stand and look alert. Don't put this strain on him all the time. After the general walk round of all the exhibits, the judge will examine each one separately. While he is doing this, or has his back to you, let your dog relax, don't keep him 'on his toes' when the judge is obviously busy elsewhere. When your turn comes, he will be all the fresher for the brief relaxation. Whether finally you get a first, second, or third, or just nothing at all, take it good-humouredly. Being a novice, you probably will, because you haven't yet learnt the correct way to call a judge blind, deaf, and senile as soon as you have walked out of the ring. This seems to be the privilege of the older hands!

(ii)

If your puppy or dog makes a promising start in his show career, persevere. Take him to all the shows you can, because no one ever makes his dog a champion by merely attending one or two shows a year. In any case, if you have some success in the beginning, this show business will get into your system and will carry you along in spite of yourself. By listening to other more experienced exhibitors, you'll very soon understand the intricacies.

It's quite a good plan to put a price on your dog in every catalogue, whether you want to sell him or not. The less you want to sell him, the better the price you can ask. There's always a chance some very rich person may come along and take a fancy to him. This may sound callous to the one-dog owner, but believe me, it's better to take a good price for any animal than to lose him through accident or illness the following week or month!

Eventually your erstwhile puppy may work up to be a champion. This means he must win three challenge certificates at three championship shows. But if he isn't a champion, if he wins (by some stroke of luck) only one challenge certificate, don't rush about in a rage and tear out your hair because he doesn't collect any more. Leave this sort of behaviour to those older and more experienced exhibitors who seem to have a flair for that kind of thing. Always be calm, philosophical, and resigned. Above all, never lose your sense of humour.

Perhaps, when your dog has become well known and has collected a number of prizes, you'll place him at stud, and insert a weekly advertisement in the dog-papers. By that time you will have learnt all about the intricacies of the canine world; but I must warn you that if he is used regularly at stud, his career as your chosen companion is over. The reason is obvious. So even if your pet is going to have a distinguished show career, why not have a bitch? You can find the best and most suitable sire and this, with a bitch who is well known in the show ring, will ensure a very handsome profit on each litter she breeds, as well as giving you the chance of keeping the best puppies for yourself. And you still have the companionship you wanted in the beginning.

Now a word about judges and judging. You, as a novice, will hear conflicting opinions on the subject. Some people will tell you that judging is, on the whole, fair. Others that it's the crookedest thing that ever happened. Books about dogs are almost monotonous in their assertions that everyone who shows a dog, be he novice or well-known kennel

172

owner, has an equal chance. It's difficult to say much, because I personally have very little interest in shows. My dogs are workers, and hardly ever see a show ring.

We'll put it this way. Mr. A has a well-known kennel, and is himself a familiar figure in his breed at all the big shows. You read about the wins of his dogs in the canine Press every week. Mr B is an unknown person who has bred a quite outstanding puppy. Experts have told him it's really superb. So Mr. B chooses a show, and takes his puppy. Mr. A is in the ring, also parading a puppy, which we all agree is not so good as Mr. B's. The judge naturally knows Mr. A. He has seen him so often. So finally Mr. A's puppy comes first, and Mr. B is either second or third or even nowhere at all. It rather depends who else is in the ring.

Now suppose, at the next show, perhaps under the same judge, Mr. A handles Mr. B's dog and vice versa, the positions of the awards may be reversed. These may be hard facts, but they are nevertheless sometimes true. I have purposely made my example a mild one, and remain silent on some of the facts which might even be harder!

There's another side to it, however, and Mr. B needn't lose heart by any means. Most judges are fair people, and quite genuinely take a dog on his merits without looking to see who is at the other end of the lead. It must be under these (and a little careful inquiry will soon find them) that Mr. B will first show his puppy. A really good animal and a lot of perseverance will always bring a final reward.

Chapter 18

DOGS OF WAR

~~~~

Since writing the foregoing reflections on you and your dog, I took part in two rather different types of training, which might be of general interest.

During the war I found myself in a large Government kennel in the Midlands, first as butcher and cook, and later as trainer among various others, most of whom had been successful obedience and trial trainers in the show world. The administration was peculiar, but I chose the job for that reason. In most Government jobs connected with the Forces, the would-be recruit had to sign an undertaking to say he would serve 'until the end of the emergency', whenever that might be. This was completely vague, and too much like prison for my taste, like signing away one's soul.

This kennel (one of several) was a branch of the Ministry of Aircraft Production. The commanding officer, who came round on inspections, was an Army colonel, a former well-known breeder of Alsatians with expert training knowledge. Our officer in charge on the spot was a flight-lieutenant of the R.A.F., and under him was a civilian head trainer. We were all civilians too, so we didn't have to sign any undertakings, except the rather curious one that we were working at our own risk, and couldn't hold our superiors responsible for any personal damage. Considering that we often had to

174

handle dogs that weren't exactly lambs, this was as peculiar as the rest of the set-up!

The way the Government went about it was also strange, but I suppose there was no alternative. Appeals were made to the public, by press and radio, to send their pet dogs of suitable breeds and sizes, or any surplus ones from breeding-kennels, to 'lend' them to the Government; these were to be trained to work in defence of aerodromes and hush-hush factories, mostly connected with the R.A.F. It produced results. People were persuaded that they were serving their country by sending their pets to be trained. Fido doing his bit seemed to appeal to them, and fresh dogs arrived at the kennels by night and day. On the whole, they settled down fairly well, with the best of food and regular work to do; but there were some elderly, pathetic animals, faithful companions, who moped and longed for their homes and masters. These were chiefly Alsatians, one-man dogs above all others.

It is obvious that if the Government had chosen a number of suitable dogs at the beginning of the war, trained and bred from the best, they could have had a reserve of properly bred young stock, without calling on the general public at all. But the British Government had never been inclined to view seriously the official employment of dogs, either with the police or in the Army. I think they probably know better now.

It has been proved beyond all doubt that properly trained dogs are a great asset and benefit to police and service personnel. Police work provides unlimited opportunities for dog auxiliaries, particularly at night. There are many occasions when a dog can far surpass a man in efficiency, and many continental police would rather leave their guns behind than forget their dogs. In patrol work, the dog may be loose or on a long rope, seeking out dark corners or alleyways for his handler, and holding up any suspicious stranger by merely barking. If the 'criminal' tries to break away, the dog follows at once and, by attacking the arm, throws him to the ground. As soon as the man is quiet, the dog merely watches him. If he is to be arrested and walked to any destination, he will never escape as long as a trained dog is one of his escorts.

At night, a dog on patrol is particularly valuable. He will pick up a human scent a long way off, and take his handler to its source. He can follow a track or trail through the thickest darkness, and is especially successful in finding any concealed loiterer, who would probably be missed by the human ear or eye, however keen. Sounds, too, are quickly picked up by a good dog, footsteps reach his ear at incredible distances. And he is taught to attack on command in all circumstances, whether his assailant is firing a gun at him or beating him with a club. Specialized tracking is another useful accomplishment a dog can perform far better than any man, and it is amazing how well the experienced dog can follow a track many hours (or even days) old, without changing to others, or being lured away by other more tempting animal scents.

Dogs have been used in Germany for identifying criminals by scent out of a row of suspects, though this is not always considered conclusive evidence. Suppose a burglar or murderer left some garment or personal possession at the scene of his crime. A dog with an average nose should be able to identify that man by connecting the scent of the object with the man who owns it; just as dogs working in obedience tests have to fetch their owner's object from a number belonging to other people. To dogs, the scent of individual human beings is unmistakable.

In the Army, dogs are used for patrolling, Red Cross work, carrying messages, and even laying telephone cables where no man could go. In all these accomplishments they are of untold value, even in these days of mechanization and H-bombs. Their general work consists of patrolling and guarding factories, aerodromes, looking for suspicious people or saboteurs round secret places. In all these tasks it should be again emphasized that the dog is often superior to his master, for his senses of sight, hearing, and scent are keyed up to a much finer pitch.

In the particular kennel where I worked, our job was to train teams of dogs up to a certain standard of general obedience. Teams consisted of eight dogs, generally the same breed, and when ready, they were moved to another kennel, where their education was completed by training for patrolling, trailing, and attack. All suitable breeds were accepted, the larger ones predominating, including great Danes, an assortment of crossbreds, sheepdogs of the working collie type, Labradors, Airedales, and Bull terriers.

Every trainer had his own row of kennels in a long corridor, for which he was responsible, washing and cleaning out, bedding, etc. Each trainer fed his own dogs from bowls of food dished up by the kitchen staff. The food mainly consisted of carcasses of condemned beef, and wholemeal bread, said to be made from condemned flour; actually a great deal of the meat was of high quality, and as long as I was at the kennel, I personally never suffered from meat rationing, as long as I could cook excellent beef steaks on the electric stove in the common-room, watched rather enviously by those who had less courage!

The job itself was not difficult, routine obedience is a simple matter, especially to people who had previously trained dogs in any way at all. There was, however, a certain amount of interest in not knowing beforehand what sort of dog you would have next, which breed, and how it would react. A batch of dogs sometimes arrived late at night, and next morning, with a leash attached to a chain collar, you would have to take out a perfectly strange dog from your kennel for exercise. He might be an Alsatian, suspicious of strangers, with bared teeth, unwilling for the chain collar to be slipped over his head. It might be a nervous Collie, who squeezed himself under the bench, and snapped at your hand as it approached with the collar. But somehow or another, you had to get the collar on and the dog out. There were one or two cases of badly shy, nervous, or savage dogs. For these, we invented a 'cat-catcher', a running noose at the end of a long stick. But, on the whole, there were not many accidents, and very few dogs that had to be destroyed as hopelessly shy or savage. (This only in the event of their owner's permission, or refusal to have them back.)

Another interesting point was in the difference between the various breeds we had to train. I mean racial character-istics as compared with those of individuals. This is a point that mightn't occur to many people, but there's no doubt that every breed of dog has its own general characteristics. It seems to me that this is a tribute (or otherwise) to the consistency of breeding to type, not only physically, but—to a remarkable degree—mentally as well. Although one has always heard general statements about the breeds—'Collies are treacherous', 'Bull terriers are fighters', and so on, I had never before realized to what extent certain characteristics belonged almost inevitably to particular breeds.

The trouble with criticizing breeds by name is that the devotees or admirers of those concerned are always inclined to work themselves into a sort of protective frenzy if their pets receive even the slightest adverse criticism. I know this, because several times I wrote magazine articles on the dogs I was training, and received a stream of letters in consequence, mainly abusive. You would imagine, reading them, that I had cast aspersions on the parentage or offspring of the writers themselves!

However, I still think these conclusions might be interesting to students of canine mentality, since they cover an experience of a great many years, previous to the war-dog training. The dogs we had at the kennel were chiefly divided into five main categories—Alsatians, Bull terriers, Airedales, sheepdogs, and crossbreds. The latter could be divided roughly into Alsatians, gun-dog and sheepdog crosses.

Of Alsatians, there is not much to say. I consider them—as I have always considered them—the cream of the whole working section of the canine race, whether their purpose is herding sheep, working with the gun, hunting men, or looking for a lost handkerchief. Dogs of varying ages came for training, but whatever the age of an Alsatian, he will learn more quickly than any other breed. Conversely, he has a long memory; his heart is more easily broken; he may pine for his home and his owner so that, although he performs to perfection, his eyes and thoughts are often far away, as though he is seeking for something he has lost. Alsatians also are more easily dealt with by people who are strangers to them, but who understand the breed.

Among the newly-arrived Alsatians, there were generally three types—the friendly, the nervous, and the savage. The last were extremely rare; among them were the silent, dangerous dogs who attacked noiselessly and without warning. The nervous ones usually calmed down after a few days, even though they would try to bite at first through sheer nervousness. The experienced trainer could generally tell at a glance to which type the dog belonged.

I never had much to do with Bull terriers until I started this general training, and had always regarded the show Bull terrier as an ugly, useless animal, bred to his fantastic appearance through the exaggerated requirements of the show ring, and thereby losing the only purpose for which he was originally intended, i.e. fighting, as well as any intelligence he may have possessed. But the Bull terrier is far from useless, though one could hardly call him hugely intelligent.

First of all, I was amazed to find that, despite his peculiar appearance, he has lost nothing of his fighting quality, a quality which was now adapted to more useful work. It might be an over-statement to say that this is all he possesses, but certainly it fills much of the small space devoted to housing his brain. The Bull terrier, show specimen or otherwise, is still very much a fighting machine, and once he has opened his eager jaws and closed them on the flesh or skin of any living thing, it would take a crowbar to open them!

The Bull terrier appears to have no reaction to physical pain, and I doubt if he ever does feel pain once his amazing emotions are really roused. Intensive training, when he has to learn to work peacefully with other dogs, does put some self-control into him, but if or when he imagines some other dog has made a face at him, he fixes his little pig-like eyes on the originator of the insult, and often his teeth chatter with the anticipation of revenge.

All the same, I have seen seven or eight of these queer animals lying in a field no more than two or three yards from one another, with their respective handlers some distance away, and managing, with admirable self-control, to stay where they are without moving for fifteen minutes or so. This is the result of training, and a very necessary one with Bull terriers. Another point about them is that you never quite know where you stand; the Bull terrier has a habit of wagging his tail and smiling broadly the moment before he bites.

The Bull terrier is extremely obstinate and stubborn. He

may be persuaded (which is doubtful) into obedience, he may be slapped sharply into lying down, but he completely refuses to be manually forced, by which I mean the more he is pushed, the more he delights in resisting with his taut, braced muscles. To me, the Bull terrier, though undoubtedly he has his uses, isn't like a dog at all; but this blind fighting spirit, when roused, shows that all the soft living or show and kennel life in the world will never take away a quality that was inherently fixed in the beginning, when his ancestors were put into the pit to tear or be torn to pieces.

If the Bull terrier is obstinate, the Airedale is wooden. On the whole, the trainers didn't like Airedales. They are slow to learn, seldom eager to work, and somewhat undisciplined in mentality, which means that they do not take kindly to law and order, but prefer to career gaily over the fields in joyful abandon. These qualities are perhaps natural in a terrier breed, and it is doubtful if they can ever be really eliminated. Many years ago I gave up breeding terriers because of this very characteristic of independence, which is, of course, liked by lots of dog-owners. The terrier has more in common with the feline tribe—he likes to be his own master, and can never for the life of him see why he should co-operate to the point of being consistently useful to his owner; this is in contrast to the herding or gun-dog breeds, which delight in pleasant co-operation.

Maybe the terrier, and especially the unfortunate show specimen, has been on the unemployment list for so long that his capacity for co-operative work has become slightly rusty. Nevertheless, this is no condemnation of the Airedale, who can be, and very often is, an excellent dog for many purposes when trained.

All sheepdogs and Collies are easily trained, but some of the Collies possess those very traits in which I used to disbelieve at one time, when I heard people say they were 'treacherous'. I don't think a sheepdog ever likes the collar and leash. Probably this comes from a very ancient instinct of the far-away days, for sheepdogs have nearly always shadowed their owners, free and unfettered. This dislike of the collar and leash is most marked in the Corgi, one of the last herding breeds to join the professional ranks. Collies may snap, generally silently, and often when the collar is being put on or taken off. On the whole, sheepdogs are inclined to be more nervous than savage.

The gun-dog breeds were sometimes represented by Labradors and Retriever crosses of various descriptions. Retrievers were, on the whole, good dogs for the purposes for which they were eventually destined in this training, provided their hearts and minds were not too much occupied by a desire to hunt game or rabbits when engaged on more important business. In fact no dog who was either gun-shy or an inveterate hunter could be accepted at all, for obvious reasons. The Labrador can be a very tough customer, and sometimes an uncertain one to train and handle. But a well-trained gun-dog of this sort was very useful, and his nose was a great asset.

Crossbreds generally were easily trained and quite suitable, provided their size came up to the required standard, and we never had much trouble with them. One incident concerning a smallish, rather insignificant Collie cross is worth repeating. A demonstration was being staged for a certain section of a Government department. One of the items in the programme took place in a car park of about two hundred cars in a large field. In one of the trucks, a man was previously hidden under a heavy tarpaulin sheet. The handler and his dog then came into the field, and the dog was sent loose to hunt for the trespasser, neither handler nor dog knowing where he would be found. In a few moments, among all those two hundred cars, the dog was scratching madly at the tarpaulin to find his man. This, needless to say, very much impressed the audience of distinguished people, who then realized that a dog is sometimes cleverer than a man.

Chapter 19

WAR DOGS AS INDIVIDUALS

People sometimes asked if the trainers ever became so attached to individual dogs that they were upset to see them go. This did happen occasionally, but on the whole, the position was a clear one from the beginning; you knew the dogs were only in transit, as it were, and so you avoided having favourites, or losing your heart to individuals. Looking back, I can only remember five or six dogs that stood out for some reason from the others I trained.

One was Peggy, the Airedale bitch. She was exceptional for her breed, and learnt her lessons very quickly and willingly. As a rule, each trainer had too many dogs for his number of kennels, and often had to keep a dog and bitch in one, and perhaps two non-fighting bitches in another, according to the space available. Peggy was first kennelled with a good-tempered Alsatian dog. She was a curious bitch, though not obviously so, and to this day I don't know why things always seemed to happen to her. She must have had the sort of character that angered other dogs, although she was very pleasant with people. But she was a bit of an exhibitionist, and would do anything to get attention. There are some people like that, and pretty tiresome they make themselves! Well, apparently Peggy did something one night that brought down the wrath of her male companion, and got badly mauled in consequence.

Peggy had to go to the sick-bay, where her torn and punctured wounds were well looked after; she was very tough and healthy, and was soon returned to me. At some inconvenience, being more than full up, I had to keep her in a kennel by herself for a bit, until she had quite recovered, but then circumstances made me cast about for another companion for her, I simply hadn't got space any longer. In my mind, I was continually trying to think out why the Alsatian had attacked her; he was such a gentle animal, completely harmless with other dogs, and it is extremely unusual for a normal dog to attack a bitch. I didn't dare put her back with him, and anyway by now he had another bitch as companion, with whom he behaved like a perfect gentleman.

So I thought I'd try her with an Alsatian of an equally nice character, in fact, almost too soft for his future job. He was long-coated, and rather striking in appearance. Peggy seemed to settle down all right for about a week, and there was no sign of trouble, except that she always bounced about jealously in the kennel when I came along, and tried to get all the attention for herself.

One morning, a thin stream of blood was running out under the kennel door when I arrived. Peggy was lying on the floor unconscious, and the dog greeted me as calmly as usual. I didn't feel like punishing him, being now sure that Peggy had brought the trouble on herself with these two different dogs. It couldn't possibly be just coincidence, there was a reason; and the reason, I felt, was that dogs were just allergic to Peggy's brand of charm.

I rushed her to the vet, and have seldom seen a dog so torn about. Among other things, she had lost an ear, a whole Airedale ear, and neither the vet nor I thought she had a chance of recovery. She was left in his infirmary, and I didn't expect to see Peggy again. But we obviously underrated her toughness; in two weeks or so, Peggy was back in my kennel, going on with her training as if nothing had happened. She looked pretty comic without her ear, and no one wanted to spoil the look of a team by sending out a one-eared Airedale. Naturally, she became perfect in the training classes, never wore a leash, and went through the complete drill with a bored nonchalance that made everyone laugh. It was not surprising that I got quite fond of her, and was sorry to see her go. She turned out to be one of the best Airedales in the team, as indeed, she should have done.

I had a favourite Bull terrier too, a coloured dog who was good enough to win in shows, and had a character all his own. He was a merry, jovial type, with a sense of humour and the most enormous energy I have ever seen. He was literally a live wire, and when he first arrived, would shoot out of the kennel door like a rocket as soon as the latch was opened, so that my first task with him was a series of lessons in self-control. In a week, he learnt to sit on his bench, one mass of quivering volcano, while I opened the door, went up to him, slipped the chain collar over his grinning face, and told him to walk to heel, which he did like a lamb, though he was just dying to gallop about the field. He had plenty of opportunity for this when we got there, and three days after, he could do it all without the leash. One couldn't help admiring the supreme self-discipline he developed after such short training. Such dogs are the ideal of all trainers, a bouncy character, well controlled, makes the best worker; far better than the soft phlegmatic individual who has to be cajoled, encouraged, and persuaded to carry out his programme. That smiling Bull terrier was also a complete non-fighter, and turned out well in his later training.

Then there was a large crossbred I disliked as much as I liked the others. He was a surly Alsatian-gun-dog cross, with a very uncertain temper. And it *was* temper, pure, bad, vicious temper. On my first day with him, he was tied up to an outside kennel, from where I had to collect him. When I went to put the chain collar on and take him for exercise, I couldn't get near him. Every device was tried, and every time I was met with bared teeth and rumbling growls.

After using a good deal of time and patience, we hadn't got any further, so I caught hold of the chain by which he was tied to the kennel with one hand, and folded the leash in the other, pulled up the chain quite short, and beat him with the leather leash. Beating was strictly discouraged, but in times like this, it was the only solution. He did his best to attack me, but hadn't enough scope on the shortened chain. In spite of sullen growls, I managed to get the collar on, and took him for a walk, during which he tried to attack me again. For dogs like this, the best answer is a foot on the leash, pinning it to the ground, so that the dog's head is kept as low as possible until he behaves himself. He really meant business, that dog, and although I did get him through his training, he seemed to have a continual and deep-seated grudge against all humans, including his handler, a grudge that had started long before he ever came to the kennel. As far as I remember, he was finally discarded when he went on to the more complicated training, as being too uncertain in temperament, attacking friend or foe without discrimination.

People who have never met this type of dog—and the ordinary person seldom does—might criticize the foregoing, and say that kind treatment would have produced better results. But it is hardly necessary to say that the dogs were approached with nothing else but kind treatment; the fact was, a suspicious surly character like this one could never have been changed. The harm had been done a long time ago, his enmity had gone too far, and only the firmest of measures would have any result. Even then, his mentality was not treacherous, but downright vicious.

We had another similar dog, a white Alsatian (I'm sorry to say!) who attacked his handler without any warning in the kennel, and bit him badly in the chest. No one could do anything with that dog, he was absolutely mean, cunning, and dangerous, and eventually had to be destroyed. Of course, in many hundreds of dogs, as with humans, there are bound to be rogues and undesirable characters, even animals of unbalanced mentality. It was our job to sort them out, to size them up, to try to understand them, and approach each individual with the right method.

One other surly dog was allotted to me, a large Boxer, the only one of his breed I ever handled in the training field. Actually, he was sickening for distemper when he came, or anyway, had contracted one of the many virus diseases that were about at the time; so he was only with me for a week or so. It was long enough for me to decide I should never do anything with him. There was no response to kindness, no sign of co-operation, and only a very unwilling obedience. As soon as his temperature rose, he went into the sickbay, and became rapidly worse. The vet was preparing an injection, and while the kennel-maid was sitting on the Boxer's bench, holding him quite gently, he turned silently and deliberately, and caught hold of her wrist.

A Boxer's jaw and teeth are no joke. The dog crunched into the girl's wrist with all the power he had, as if it were a chicken carcass, and remained grinding the bones for many seconds before two or three people could prise his jaws open. He died soon after, but the girl's arm and bones were affected, and went septic, and for years after she had to have treatment. In fact, I believe the arm never really recovered.

Of the individuals I remember with the greatest pleasure was a small Collie bitch of the working type; she was more or less mine for a very long time, owing to an accident. The latter was one that happens in the best of households; she had managed to get pregnant, no one knew how, as all precautions were continually taken to prevent such events. However, there she was, at the end of her short training (she was exceptionally intelligent), with a guilty bulging stomach. There was nothing to do but keep her till she whelped. All but one of the puppies were destroyed, and that one given away as soon as possible.

Meanwhile, she was my star turn, in fact, the star turn of the kennel. She knew her lessons backwards, and the leash was not for her. So perfect was her performance, and she obviously loved working so much, that I am sure she would have won well in obedience classes. But the day came when she too went off with a team, and I really missed her more than I can say. What a lovely temperament the working Collie has! Absolutely devoted, loyal, incorruptible. In my own standard of the breeds, the working Collie certainly comes third to Alsatians and Corgis; and perhaps even equal second with the Corgis, who are not always devoid of tantrums!

Our work during the war was not without results. Dogs have been officially recognized for certain tasks since then, with the Army, Air Force, and Police, which is all to the good. But there was one aspect of the system of our time which seemed very wrong, and would have never been necessary if the Government had kept and bred their own dogs. That was the handing back, when the war was over.

At the risk of being unpopular, I should like to suggest that the man in the street is not nearly as knowledgeable about dogs and their management as he should be. The enthusiasm for keeping a dog as a pet is most natural, and

189

the majority of people have it. But the would-be owner of a pet often selects an entirely unsuitable breed. A number of reasons account for this. Perhaps he goes to a dog show, and is absolutely fascinated by the obedience work of Alsatians or Dobermanns. In his enthusiasm, he decides to have a puppy of such a breed. Maybe he has admired a lively Boxer playing in the park, or even fallen for a Rottweiler because of its size and appearance.

So he gets his puppy, and is well satisfied until it grows up, and develops bad habits—kills cats, bites children, or savages sheep, according to circumstances and environment. That brings disillusionment to the owner, he is disheartened with his chosen breed, not realizing that the adverse developments are all his own fault, which is what I have been trying to show in this book.

Most breeds of dogs have been evolved with a purpose. Many of them have been bred with as much thought for their mental powers as their physical strength or appearance. Among the latter are Bull mastiffs, Alsatians, Boxers, Rottweilers, Dobermanns, and most of the ordinary working breeds—sheepdogs, gun-dogs, even Dachshunds. Some have nowadays lost their original purpose, Borzois have ceased to hunt wolves, and Great Danes to chase boars. But it is as well to remember the purpose of the others when considering a choice of pet.

As I have already indicated several times, the purely hound and herding dogs are nearly always suitable as pets, they are adaptable and generally kindly natured. But the breeds that have been developed and used for hunting men, guarding property, catching evil-doers, and helping to keep law and order, should be very carefully considered before they are adopted as pets. The owner of such dogs should know what he is doing, and be able to cope with that kind of temperament and its requirements.

190

Dogs that have been bred for work of a highly specialized kind nearly always have a tireless physique and an equally energetic brain. They must have something to do, something to occupy body and mind. They will not thrive on a life of ease, of too little exercise, physical and mental. They want a job, and their energies must be put into some useful activity; or they will find their own doubtful pursuits, like those I have mentioned, and the owner will soon be in trouble.

This lack of training knowledge in many owners of dogs of this kind has frequently brought the breeds into disrepute, quite without justification. When the idle member of a working breed goes off—probably with an equally idle and un-supervised friend—to chase and savage sheep, or pull boys off bicycles, the fault is entirely and completely with the owner, not with the breed of dog.

Boxers, for instance, are handsome, attractive, sound, and full of energy. The puppies are comical and tempting. But I always remember that during the war, there was a trained Boxer in the Middle East, who in a few years had nine deaths and one hundred and thirty-four arrests to his credit. His credit—yes indeed, a fine performance, but unless you know something about training and controlling dogs, then why not keep a Cocker spaniel or a Corgi?

Rottweilers are equally handsome in their own rugged way, but rugged is a suitable term for them. In Germany, they have been fearsome and feared guards for generations, and are used as highly trained police dogs. The same applies to Dobermanns, whose characters are more lively and restless. Alsatians often seem fated to get into the wrong hands, and for many years in England they had a bad reputation that was never justified.

But for anyone who can't resist these breeds, there is now always the opportunity to join organized obedience classes, so general in England and America. That is the solution, and a good healthy one it is.

The idea of handing back after the war the individuals among those breeds who had been deliberately trained to attack humans always seemed to me to be quite beyond sense. It wasn't likely that when Rex the Alsatian or Bill the Bull terrier returned to their fond owners, the latter would at once take a course in handling potential man-hunters. The whole scheme was wrong in theory, but I have to admit I heard of no particular incidents as a result of this.

Let us hope it will never happen again. The breeding and training of dogs for wartime services should never depend on the borrowing of private pets.

Chapter 20

FILM TRAINING

~

For various reasons that don't belong here, I left the Government kennels, and went to an agricultural job in a Midlands hostel, where my friend Helen and I produced vegetables, and generally looked after the grounds. Soon after we started on this, I had a letter out of the blue that further increased the scope of our activities. A film producer, who had read one of my training articles in a magazine, wrote that he was looking for someone who could train and work a dog to take part in a war film, specially written for a canine star. Could I suggest a dog and someone suitable to train it? This was too good to be handed on elsewhere, and though I had no dog, and was pretty busy in the gardening job, I replied that I would certainly find a dog, and would myself train it to do whatever was wanted.

This was followed by an interview in London, where I read quickly through the script, and thought it would be quite feasible. The producer told me to let him know when I had a dog, and began the training. He handed me an advance cheque, the sum of which seemed too good to be true.

Then came the greatest piece of luck. I advertised for a white Alsatian bitch, with a pedigree containing as much of my own strain as possible. As a result I was offered a bitch from the last litter I bred in the beginning of the war, now about three years old, and completely untrained. I clinched the deal with a telegram, and Helen and I prepared a kennel in one of the hostel's air-raid shelters, a roomy hut near our own quarters. We were in the greatest excitement when we went to fetch Wanda from the station. There she was, a small grubby-looking bitch, tied to a lamp-post, curled up in a peevish ball, and growling at us when we went to undo the chain.

But very soon I found Wanda was everything I had hoped for and dreamed about when I planned the mating that produced her; I lost no time in starting to train her, first in general obedience, and then with a view to things she had to do in the story. It was lucky I had an experienced partner, or it would have been much more difficult. One person had to do the handling and commands, the other take the part of the actors in the various scenes. It was unbelievably good to have a dog again, and the manager of the hostel was not only agreeable, but most interested in the whole project.

Dogs and animals in films may look as if they are acting spontaneously and naturally, but nothing is further from the truth. Every single move is the result of long training, patience, and timing; when you think how difficult it is to get any sort of successful picture of your own pets, it can be realized how much more trouble has to be taken in a full-length film. Every scene had to be continually rehearsed and perfected, probably more with an animal than with human actors. Moreover, the element of boredom and staleness has to be considered far more with a trained dog than with humans, as you can't explain to a dog the importance of the occasion.

In the beginning, we had an unexpected problem, one I had so far hardly ever met in any of my Alsatians. Wanda had no idea of retrieving, no desire to play with or carry a

194

ball, and she refused to pick up anything, even in play. This was quite serious, because naturally, during the story, she had to carry various objects; the film began with the dog running off with a girl's shoe. I had to resort to the method advised in this book, and go about the training the long, hard way. That was by opening Wanda's mouth, and putting the ball or shoe between her jaws, every time with the same command. Gradually she opened her mouth herself on hearing the command, and by degrees came to the stage of picking the object up from the ground. Later, she did that at increasing distances, until she was as competent and sure as any other retriever.

More than that, she came to adore ball games, and developed a healthy passion for running after the ball, just as all my old dogs used to do. Also, she soon had a companion to compete with her, and make her all the keener. The way this came about was rather amusing. A long time before, I had sold a Corgi puppy as a pet to some people in London. They wrote to me while I was at the hostel, in great distress, saying they had lost it with distemper, and could I get them another? I asked a breeder to send me an eight-week-old puppy, but when Flossie arrived, she was so small and so cute, and had such a comical character, that Helen and I couldn't bear to send her away again. So a substitute was despatched to London, and Flossie remained with us, sharing Wanda's air-raid shelter.

Wanda went everywhere with us, always loose. She had a real film-star mentality, and loved to be the centre of attraction. She followed close to heel in the thickest crowds, sat and waited patiently outside shops, and her favourite enjoyment was riding on the top story of a double-decker bus. Here she was supposed to lie down beside us, and not get in anyone's way. But soon she would worm off, sometimes on her stomach, down the passage between the seats, until she came to someone who was really sympathetic (not like the harsh people she had the misfortune to live with!); she would then stand, leaning against the delighted stranger, gazing into his face as though she would never love anyone else, looking back from time to time at us with a supercilious expression that was so funny we always had to laugh. In the end, we let her please herself, and she paced the passage regularly, making friends all the way. Thinking back, I don't believe I ever had an Alsatian I liked more. Wanda was not handsome, but she had everything, including the most expressive dark eyes that shone like ebony.

She was already insured for a very large sum, and a contract was to be signed later for two or three subsequent films. The prospects looked fairly rosy, and the training progressed every day. Wanda loved it, being a complete exhibitionist of the nicest sort, and was always on her toes for the next lesson. Unlike other feminine stars of whom we sometimes hear, she was not temperamental and had no tantrums. But suddenly an awful thought came to us— suppose anything happened to Wanda, suppose she was run over, or had an accident? It was unthinkable, of course, but we had to face it. The answer was to try to find a substitute, an understudy.

I advertised again, and once more was lucky in finding a white bitch, younger and better-looking than Wanda; but her character wasn't the same, and she didn't learn so easily. Still, it made us feel more comfortable, and we taught her the routine drill. Thus Della joined the other two in the air-raid shelter, and sometimes we gave a demonstration on Sundays to the kindly manager of the hostel, without whose permission and co-operation we couldn't have got very far.

There were several specialized tricks Wanda had to do in the story. One was to slip her collar when she was being 'kidnapped', and escape at full speed. She had to do this at a particular moment, while the 'villain' who had her on the leash was talking to someone else. Slipping a collar is not something you want your dog to learn, but everything must be sacrificed to art; or—to be more honest—to the rich rewards art sometimes brings! By now, nearly all Wanda's training was based on her keenness to work with the ball. For the slipping-collar act, we first put on a very loose leather collar, attached to a leash. While she was watching, the other handler, at a fair distance, would throw the ball so that Wanda could see where it went. At the command 'Fetch it!' Wanda strained on the leash, and the handler pulled the collar over her head to help her escape.

By degrees, the collar was fastened tighter, and Wanda got used to pulling her head backwards out of it with a lightning movement. The advantage of the ball was to make her eager, and to be able to control the exact moment of escape, which was only on the command to fetch. When the trick was perfected, it looked most realistic, especially as I later gave the command by signal. In fact, most of the work was carried out by signs in the end, so that interference with any sound-recording was eliminated.

Another item I didn't enjoy teaching her was that of standing on her hind-legs, and stealing a joint of meat from a table. Just imagine any decent, civilized dog doing that! Naturally, it was taught easily enough, but it always went against the grain with me, though Wanda performed it with obvious enjoyment and satisfaction. (No, we didn't use a real joint of meat in rationed wartime England!)

Then there was the trick of reviving the airman who had crashed. She had to turn him over with her nose or paws, or both, lick his face, and generally render the canine version of first aid. This we also taught her with the ball, once she relished the idea of always getting hold of it. The 'airman' first sat on the ground, Wanda standing by the handler a little way off. She was told to stay, while the handler threw the ball to the airman, who concealed it in 'his' shirt, and then lay down in the correct position. Wanda was told to get the ball, and her movements while she was violently trying to reach it were most realistic, both with nose and paws. The final ceremony of licking the face was reserved for a close-up shot, and was made easy by minute pieces of liver concealed around the neck and collar of the unfortunate airman, with a bit or two hidden in his ears for good measure!

This use of the ball gave all Wanda's movements a quickness and snap that were very effective. But there was a moment in the story when she had to be footsore, weary, lame, and at the end of her tether—the sort of time in the film when all the handkerchiefs come out, real good sob stuff. Curiously enough, this was one of her most talented performances, and a cause of pride to her trainer. First, I had a fast and tiring ball game with her, to produce the necessary state of panting. Then I told her to stand and stay, while I walked a long way off, and turned round, facing her. At the command 'Come slowly', she drooped her head and tail, and crept along towards me, the picture of utter dejection. During this slow progress, I sometimes made her lie down, sometimes sit, always looking the soul of lost misery. Towards the end of this heart-rending walk, she slowly lay on her side, legs stretched cut, practically at the point of death. It would have brought tears to the eyes of the strongest man.

Many times I showed this trick to various people, and it really did astonish them. The funny thing was that Wanda adored doing it, probably because of the lavish applause she knew it brought. Occasionally, just to show the audience that this misery was entirely an act, I called her in an ordinary, loud, cheerful voice, and at once she came bounding along at her fastest pace, smiling all over. In the actual shots of this scene, I planned to tie two toes together with thin twine, which would have given a perfect temporary lameness.

When I first read the script, I saw at once the greatest difficulty of all, which was an act essential to the whole story, and had to take place on many occasions and different places. Wanda had to dislike the 'villain' so much that every time she saw him, she had to charge at and chase him, and finally tear out the seat of his pants; the last occasion was inside a court-room. This seemed an insurmountable problem at first, because I had the alternative of teaching her really to hate and attack whoever the villain was, or see if I could get round the situation some other way. Luckily, as we developed the play with the ball until it had become a ruling passion with her, the solution was not so difficult.

I got hold of an old golf-ball, which she soon liked as much as the larger rubber one. First I wrapped it in a handkerchief, which I threw to Helen, who ran away with it in her hand. Wanda was told to fetch it. She chased the hand holding the hidden ball, and after a few jumps, it was given to her, so that she could bring it back to me. This developed further. The ball, still in a rag or handkerchief, was put loosely in an obvious position, hanging from the back of Helen's belt. I first showed Wanda where it was, and when Helen ran away, gave the order to retrieve. She made a convincing chase, and pulled the whole thing away from the belt.

From this stage it was all quite easy. The ball was placed farther up, under a coat, and secured rather more tightly. Wanda still pulled it away, still enjoyed the chase. I planned in the actual shots to have a similar arrangement, but a patch of trouser, previously cut out and fixed loosely to the trouser seat, attached to the ball, invisible under the coat. It would have been most effective.

After we had reached a satisfactory stage in all this training, the director (as distinct from the producer) in London wanted to see how things were going. On one of our free days we went off by train, accompanied by the star and her understudy, and met the director, producer, and author in Regent's Park for a demonstration. It was winter, bitterly cold, with a freezing wind. Our film employers looked the part, and wore town overcoats, collars turned up to the ears. We had just started on our repertoire, according to the copy of the script, when a snowstorm came on. Undaunted and quite confident, we struggled on for five minutes, more concerned with what we were doing than the blizzard now whistling about the park; and as we had just completed what we thought was a most satisfactory performance, we looked up and saw the tail ends of our film company disappearing into a taxi!

However, they appeared to be satisfied; the arrangements went on, and the training, until Wanda knew it all by heart, and we only had a refresher course once a week. There seemed to be a lot of delay, but I had no grumbles as long as the cheques kept coming. All I heard was that the producer would be ready any time soon for preliminary shooting, to see how things looked on the screen. We were planning a campaign to prove this work was necessary for the satisfaction of the Labour Exchange, who ruled everyone's lives at that time; because, as soon as the business started in earnest, we should give up gardening.

Meanwhile, the war had become more serious, the bombing more widespread. You never saw Wanda in her picture? No, because there wasn't any picture. After the V rockets began to burst all over the outskirts of London, the film was called off. The last I heard of the director was that he had taken up temporary residence in the remoter part of Wales. We never saw him again.

CONCLUSION

—◆—

Will you forgive me, I wonder, if I leave for a moment this talk of training and kennelling, feeding and ailments? I should like to forget the check-cord and collar, food-bowl and showring. Rather I would wander slowly back through more than thirty years, a reluctant journey that holds a tightening of the heart, a sigh or two, and some very precious memories. Back to an immense stableyard, flanked by tall beeches and the slender silver birch, where the sun shone as it never seems to shine now, and poor old blind Paddy was the first dog we ever knew. There was Rattler the Airedale, old as Paddy, grim fighter, scarred and grey. Paddy was blind with age; Rattler's sightless eye was the legacy of his warlike nature. Yes, and Fidget, Buck, Gypsy, Bill, and many others whose unforgotten lives are told elsewhere.

Let me remember again a small, aggressive, and rather bloodthirsty child hunting a pack of terriers through the fields and gorse by a blue sea, armed with a crop and a store of bad language that seemed somehow to control this wild and motley gathering. And the village dogs who came at full speed to the shrill whistle which always meant a day's hunting. Those litters of puppies, importantly bred from working terriers by the small owner. Of course they had no equal, they were better than anyone else's puppies! And the mistaken inspiration of genius that imagined a fox-terrier mated with a bulldog (brindled) would produce pure bull-terriers to be sold at immense profit!

Let me remember it all, even though some of it seems to hurt so much. . . . Stray dogs, stray memories, moving right up to the present when only last year I shot two promising puppies suffering from an incurable and terrible illness. The third—the best—the hearty one with a tail that flogged his flanks in the joy of living, the one who was always laughing, I thought he surely would recover, he was so strong. . . . But later, when I went to take him out of the box for the last time, his lively tail could only raise a faint little thump of welcome—and farewell. And Sally. . . .

Why twist the knife? It's always farewell. Ridiculous sentimentality, of course; dogs are only animals. Yet allow me my moment of digression, forgive me while I remember in silence so many, too many small graves beside the road of those long years. . . .

My dogs, past and present, who have taught me the little I know. To whom, after all, I owe so much.

INDEX